STILL FIGHTING *for* GEMMA

STILL FIGHTING *for* GEMMA

SUSAN D'ARCY AND ROB EDWARDS

BLOOMSBURY

First published in Great Britain 1995
Bloomsbury Publishing Plc, 2 Soho Square, London W1V 6HB

A CIP catalogue record for this book is
available from the British Library

ISBN 0 7475 2186 7

10 9 8 7 6 5 4 3 2 1

Typeset by Hewer Text Composition Services, Edinburgh
Printed in Great Britain by Clays Ltd, St Ives plc

For Gemma, Jamie, Amy and Kerry

Thou art a soul in bliss; but I am bound
Upon a wheel of fire, that mine own tears
Do scald like molten lead.

William Shakespeare, *King Lear*

Contents

Foreword

It is late in the evening. I am sitting at my kitchen table drinking a cup of coffee. Steven, my husband, is watching television in the living room. My two children, Richenda and Samina, are asleep upstairs. Outside it is dark and cold; in here, cosy and warm. It is the first time I have been on my own all day. I am thinking.

I am sitting here for a purpose. In front of me is a new pad of lined paper; in my hand, a pen. I have a story to tell. It has, I think, some moments of joy, some moments of pain and some moments of anger. But I hope that, by the end, it will be the anger that will linger. For I do not put pen to paper to entertain or to depress, but to ignite. I do not count myself amongst those who are prepared to sit back and just accept everything that life throws at them. I believe that if something is wrong, we all have to take responsibility for righting it. I believe that if crimes are committed – no matter how strong and cruel the criminal – we should all do what we can to seek justice. I believe, fundamentally, that we must fight.

This book is about my fight. It is a fight that has determined most of my adult life, and I fully expect it will continue to do so. It is a fight fuelled from deep within my being. In its course so far I have argued with my husband, my family, my community. I have done battle with social security officials, teachers, doctors, nurses, fund-raisers, lawyers, journalists and television producers. Most importantly of all, I have taken on one of the most powerful and dangerous of opponents – the nuclear industry. How it all began, I will tell. How I fared, you will learn. Whether I was right, you will judge.

There will doubtless be some who will dismiss what I say as emotional, as if that somehow renders it irrelevant. In the fierce dispute about the wisdom or otherwise of nuclear power, defining an opponent – particularly a woman – as emotional is seen by some pro-nuclear scientists as the clinching argument. What I have to say is certainly emotional, but unashamedly so. Emotions are the very stuff of life. I have feelings, sometimes overwhelmingly powerful ones, that influence my actions. They inform my opinions, affect my judgements and guide my beliefs. They do not diminish my life, but enrich it. I suspect it is exactly the same with every other human being on this planet. If the nuclear enthusiasts do not accept that they have an emotional attachment to their technology, they are deluding themselves. If they really believe that their expert opinions are somehow clinically detached from their feelings, they are denying their humanity.

That does not imply, of course, the abandonment of rational argument. I hope there will be plenty of that in what follows, founded in historical and demonstrable fact. For that, and for much else, I am grateful to Rob Edwards, who is helping to transform my handwritten ramblings into a coherent and, I hope, easily readable narrative. Our aim is to be fair, honest and accurate. Although as a matter of style the book will be written throughout in the first person, it is in reality a genuine joint effort. Rob, who has had to live through by proxy what I lived through in person, is my co-author and not my ghost-writer.

I am just an ordinary woman. I have had little formal education. I have never had much money. If events had turned out differently, no one outside of my immediate family and friends would ever have heard of me. But something happened that changed the course of my life. It put my name in the newspapers and my face on the television, and ultimately led to an actress playing my part in a drama-documentary seen by eight million people in Britain. Believe me, if I could live my life over again, I would rather that I had not become famous. I would have preferred to have remained happily unknown.

But now that is not an option, and I have to write this book. The act of writing will, I am sure, help ease the pain, help perform some kind of emotional catharsis. But that is not the reason I am at the kitchen table, thinking, and will be for countless evenings to come. I am here for someone special. She is nudging my elbow, whispering in my ear, smiling through my tears. Her ghostly presence haunts this room, and every room in this house. Her face is at every window, her touch in every movement, her voice in every echo. If I close my eyes, I can see her running in from the garden, head thrown back, laughing, just as if it were yesterday. I can still feel her embrace.

I'm here, Gemma, I'm here.

ACKNOWLEDGEMENTS

It is doubtful whether this book would have ever been written had it not been for our mutual friend James Cutler, who put us in touch with each other. The fight which it describes might never have begun had it not been for Martyn Day and his colleagues, particularly Susan Wilde, Richard Meeran and Jenny Cooksey, who have helped us remember what happened. We are grateful in various other ways to Janine Allis-Smith, Benita Edzard, Martin Forwood, Ingrid Hansen, Frances Hardy, Allison Harkins, Alke Langemann, David Lowry, David Reynolds, Pete Roche, Mike Townsley, Simon Trewin, Rosie Waterhouse, Barry Wigmore and others whom we cannot name.

For immeasurable support, strength and solace over the years we thank Alison; Cindy, Les and Lesley; Denise and Steve; Helen and John; Ian, Kay and Victoria; Janet and Denise; Kevin and Diane; Lynn and Ronald; Stan and June; Tracy; Wendy and Cyril; all the staff on Ward 16 South of the Royal Victoria Infirmary in Newcastle; and all our families, far and near. The debt of love we owe to those most close to us – Lindsay, Robyn and Fiona; Russell, Tina, Samina, Richenda and Steven – is beyond words.

Chapter 1

The Contaminated Shore

I suppose – to put it politely – I was always a rebel, a product of wild blood mixing. My father was born in 1929 in a small Italian farming village called Picenza, near Milan. His family was large, Catholic and never had much money, but they survived by always helping each other out. As a young man he came to England in 1951, despite speaking virtually no English, to join his brother working in the Cumbrian iron ore mines. He left after a while to go and work in a friend's café in the East End of London, which is where he met my mother. She was born in 1939 and survived a tough upbringing in the East End, most of it spent in children's homes. They both had to work hard for a living.

My father returned to the ore mines in 1959, settling in Cleator Moor in Cumbria. Then, as now, it was a long, thin, grey-stone town perched on the windswept but majestic north-west edge of the Lake District, no more than five miles from the coast. It was also – although no one thought much about it at the time – just eight miles from a nuclear reprocessing complex then known as Windscale, now as Sellafield. When my father's sister-in-law became ill, he rang my mother and asked if she would come up to Cleator Moor to help look after her. She agreed, and in January 1961 they were married. My elder sister, Santina, now always known as Tina, was born within the year. Eighteen months later – on 4 March 1963 at 121 Berks Road, Cleator Moor – I started life as Susan Lena Albertelli. When I was three the family emigrated to Italy, but my mother quickly became homesick and so we all moved back to England, to London's East End. There my father worked for a brewery in Whitechapel and my mother took on countless cleaning jobs, which I remember helping her with.

Tina and I went to school in London, but we successfully played truant for months at a time. My mother suffered a nervous breakdown, which as a child I found very difficult to handle. Then in 1974, when I was eleven, my father was made redundant. Tina and I, who had been on holiday to Cumbria and fallen in love with the place, begged our parents to return there. So with his redundancy money my father bought a cheap house in Cleator Moor, the community in which we have lived ever since. Growing up amidst the beautiful hills, lakes and beaches of Cumbria seemed very different from the streets of London: much calmer and safer. I remember thinking that Cumbrian children seemed to have all the time in the world. When Tina was fifteen she met her future husband, Russell, who worked as a chef in a busy hotel in Keswick. At sixteen she left school and went to work as a chambermaid in the same hotel, leaving me at home with my parents.

Like most teenagers, I started going out: drinking, smoking, bluffing my way into pubs and clubs, and meeting boys. My mother, much to her surprise, became pregnant again and gave birth to Nina, my younger sister. I left school at sixteen with no exam passes and went to work in a local fish factory, shelling crayfish to make them into scampi. It was not a glamorous job, and I had to shower for ages after work to get rid of the smell. But for a girl as young as I was, the money was good, and I loved eating scampi. After that I was a chambermaid for a short while, then a factory hand making plugs. I was still sixteen when I met Steven D'Arcy at a local nightclub. He had been going out with a girl who lived opposite us and, because I fancied him, I suggested to her that she should stay with her other boyfriend. Steven, a quiet, good-looking, self-effacing nineteen-year-old Liverpudlian with a wicked sense of humour, was working for a contractor at Sellafield. For better or for worse, he has stuck with me ever since.

Around the same time I became pregnant. My father, to put it mildly, was not pleased, but eventually had to accept that I was going to have the baby. Steven, who stood by me throughout, came to live with me, and on 27 July 1980 Richenda Maria D'Arcy was born. She was two months premature, weighing just 2lb 6oz at birth, and had to spent most of her first month in a hospital incubator. But she was a very beautiful baby – dainty, with dark skin and jet-black hair. Steven and I were given a council house close to my parents, where we took Richenda and tried to become adults. It was not easy. Steven had lost his job at Sellafield and we had no idea how to manage money, so we kept running into debt and asking my father to bail us out. I decided to go back to work as a crayfish sheller, leaving Steven at home to look after Richenda. In 1981 Steven and I were married and I became Susan D'Arcy.

The strain of having to bring up an unexpected third child soon told on my parents, who decided after twenty-three years of marriage that they had had enough of each other. My mother went back to London on her own, leaving little Nina with my father. He had got a job with a contractor at Sellafield, so when he was at work Nina came to Tina's or my house. Tina and Russell had a little boy, Nikki, born a year after Richenda, and we often all used to go out together. One of our favourite outings was to the seaside, either to St Bees or to one of the many other Cumbrian beaches. We would go in all weathers to watch the waves – the stormier the better – and Steven would take lots of photographs.

When Richenda was two, Steven and I decided to have another baby. He had started work at Sellafield again, and our financial outlook was more promising. We conceived a child on 4 March 1983. This time the announcement that I was pregnant was greeted with great joy by all our families, especially Richenda. For myself I had never been happier, particularly when I discovered that Tina was expecting her second child too. We hoped that both our second children could become playmates and keep each other company in the same way as Richenda and Nikki had done. Tina and I had always been very close and loved doing everything together. We never lived more than a few hundred yards apart. Despite the fact that she was eighteen months older than me, we looked, felt and acted the same. She usually wears her hair longer than me, but otherwise we could be twins. Sometimes we have been mistaken for each other.

The spring and summer of my pregnancy were lovely. I spent long hours every week on the beaches – sand between my toes, salt spray on my lips – walking, sitting, staring, playing. We took picnics there, we played in the swing parks, we explored the rock pools, we paddled in the shallows. We built sandcastles and sand-boats, we dug huge holes, we buried each other – all the things that families usually do on beaches. Invariably we would all end up with sand in every orifice – in our ears, in our noses, in our hair. When it was warm enough, I swam in the sea, and felt my skin prickle from the salt when I dried. Even when autumn came and I had grown quite large, we still went down there for regular walks.

In November 1983, two days before the baby was due, I saw on the television news that the local environmental group Cumbrians Opposed to a Radioactive Environment (C.O.R.E.) was putting up danger signs on the beaches warning of radioactive contamination from Sellafield. The site's operator, British Nuclear Fuels Limited (BNFL), accused C.O.R.E. of scaremongering and insisted that the coast was quite safe. The next day, to see what all the fuss was about, we went down to the beach. Nine months pregnant, I stood and stared at a sign emblazoned with a skull and crossbones, puzzled as to what it really meant. That evening I went into hospital to have the baby induced. On television in the ward day-room, I saw that the government was now warning people not to use the beaches because they had in fact been contaminated with radioactive waste. But at the time it was difficult to understand what on earth was going on, and in any case I had other things on my mind.

It was not until much later that I learned exactly what had happened. A team of divers from the environmental group Greenpeace, working from a dinghy off the Cumbrian coast, had been trying to block Sellafield's underwater discharge pipe. When they emerged from the water, Greenpeace's geiger counters revealed that they were seriously contaminated. It was only when the organisation publicised this fact that British Nuclear Fuels admitted that they had been having problems with their radioactive discharges. Because of a breakdown in communication between shifts, 170,000 gigabecquerels (a very large unit of radioactivity) of what was officially termed 'radioactive crud' had been wrongly diverted into a tank in which effluent was being prepared for discharge into the sea. Once there it could not be removed, so at the beginning of November Sellafield managers had decided to flush it out to sea. There it formed a uniquely unpleasant radioactive slick which seriously polluted much of the Cumbrian coast. It was probably clinging to the beaches along which I walked while heavily pregnant.

Shortly after the incident BNFL closed the beach at Seascale for twenty-four hours, but then declared it safe and opened it again. A few days later, on 30 November 1983, while I was being induced in hospital, the Department of the Environment warned the public not to use the fifteen-mile stretch of shoreline either side of Sellafield 'for the time being' because of the dangers to health posed by the radioactive flotsam that was being washed ashore. The advice stayed in force for a full six months, until a junior Energy Minister, Giles Shaw, took a well-publicised fifteen-minute swim in the sea off Seascale beach, supposedly showing that it was safe again.

In retrospect BNFL admitted that it had made a 'very serious error', but insisted that it was an 'isolated incident'. In fact there had been at least three other past occasions on which beaches had been specifically polluted. In 1961 radioactive liquid leaked from an evaporator and polluted part of the beach near Sellafield. In 1964 the clean-out of a waste tank sent water and accumulated radioactive sludge out to sea in breach of permitted discharge limits. In December 1976, the government revealed that radioactive tritium had been discovered on Cumbrian beaches, probably from a nuclear waste store. The November 1983 contamination, though, was by far the most serious, and provoked one of the worst crises in Sellafield's history.

No fewer than three official reports were produced on the incident, the first by the Ministry of Agriculture, Fisheries and Food, the second by the Department of the Environment's Radiochemical Inspectorate, and the third by the government's Nuclear Installations Inspectorate. The first concluded that the discharge would not harm human health unless people handled contaminated debris. The second criticised BNFL for 'apparent deficiencies' and recommended twenty-five improvements in procedures. The third made a further eight recommendations and concluded that better operating procedures would have prevented the shore from becoming contaminated. Six months later it was announced that the Director of Public Prosecutions was taking the unprecedented step of prosecuting BNFL for alleged breaches of its safety licence. In June 1985 the company appeared in court charged with two offences under the 1960 Radioactive Substances Act and four under the 1965 Nuclear Installations Act. After a three-day trial, BNFL was fined £10,000 and found guilty on four counts: failing to keep discharges 'as low as reasonably achievable'; failing to minimise exposure of people to radiation; failing to keep adequate records of marine discharges; and failing to keep adequate records of operations.

This, then, was the situation when my second child, another girl, was delivered by Caesarian section, after showing signs of stress during labour, at 11.58 a.m. on 30 November 1983. She weighed 5lb 12oz and, after Richenda, looked huge at birth. We all fell instantaneously in love with her, and her arrival was warmly welcomed by both Steven's family and my own. Steven wanted to call her Emily, but I decided on Donna Louise and registered her in that name. For six weeks we called her Donna until, on a visit to Steven's relatives in Liverpool, we all agreed that it just did not suit her. Steven still talked about Emily, or Emma, and then someone – I can't remember who – suggested Gemma. On the way home I was sitting in the back of the car cradling her in my arms and murmuring, 'Gem, our little gem.' From that moment on she has been known as Gemma, or, as she later liked to describe herself, Gemma Donna Louise D'Arcy.

Three months later Tina gave birth to her own second child,

another girl, whom she named Bianca. She was a beautiful baby like Richenda, dark-skinned, dark-haired and obviously Italian. But Gemma was different. She was pale, virtually bald at the beginning and nothing like as attractive as her sister or cousin. When Tina and I took the new arrivals out together in their prams, people would say how beautiful Bianca looked, especially as she was usually asleep. Then they would look at Gemma, stuffing a biscuit into her mouth, her nose running, her face filthy, and smile thinly. Tina and I used to laugh because they looked so funny side by side.

I only breast-fed Gemma for the first two weeks because she developed a rash on her neck which the health visitor said could have been an allergic reaction to my milk. But she fed well on powdered baby's milk, then cow's milk, then solids, growing chubby and strong. As she became bigger, she began to change from an ugly duckling into a swan. Her hair grew mousey-brown, very fine and straight. Her eyes became light golden brown – although one, if you looked closely, was half green. She had a perfect nose, small and rounded. Her face, always fair, produced dense crops of freckles in the summer. Thankfully, she never cried very much. My abiding memory is of her crawling around the floor at about a year old, grinning like a Cheshire cat. She sensed when we were feeling sad, and sometimes tried to cheer us up by making funny noises or expressions. She had inherited her father's crazy and sometimes cruel sense of humour and was often mischievous, although nearly always with a grin. Like many second children, she developed a tough, determined personality designed to make sure that she always got her fair share of parental attention.

When, at fourteen months, she started walking on her own, there was no stopping her. More than anything, she loved going outdoors to play. One day when I was hanging out the washing in the back garden I heard the elderly lady who lived next door shouting. I turned round to see Gemma raiding her strawberry patch. I fetched her back into our garden, apologising to the lady – who later came across to give Gemma some 'official' strawberries.

When she was eighteen months old, she gave us our first major fright. Steven tripped while carrying her upstairs and she fell on her nose. He took her into hospital where she was X-rayed with a lead bib to check whether her nose was broken. Thankfully, it just turned out to be badly bruised. The only other time she went into hospital during her first three years was when she pushed a bead right up her nose. It had to be extracted with tweezers.

The health visitor was at one point sufficiently worried about her speech development to arrange an appointment for her to see a speech therapist. Given that she was not yet two years old, I thought this was stupid and put the appointment card in the rubbish bin. Again, like many second children, she was a little slower than Richenda in learning to talk. But talk she soon did – endlessly, bossily and with a strong Cumbrian accent. Because of all the running around she did outside she was generally fit and healthy, neither too fat nor too thin. Her young limbs, as they gradually extended, seemed supple and strong. She grew tall for her age, often being mistaken for an older child. But she always remained pale, so much so that we nicknamed her 'the milk bottle'.

As Tina and I had hoped, she and her cousin, Bianca, became good friends. They spent hours together every day, laughing, playing, quarrelling and making up. Gemma would always try and be the boss, but often Bianca, who had a strong will of her own too, would not have it. Soon there were new playmates, too. After Gemma had turned three, we moved to a bigger council house closer to the centre of Cleator Moor. I started work again at a local packaging company called Mardons Composites, which makes the cardboard tubes for whisky bottles. Gemma made friends with the identical twins from next door, one called Julie and the other called – confusingly – Gemma. Their mother, Helen, became a close friend of mine. Her elder daughter, Kerry, had a birthday on the day next to Gemma's and became a friend of Richenda's. My Gemma was very good at telling the twins apart, which I was not, and the three of them became as thick as thieves. She used to mother them and, I think, teach them a few bad habits.

There was one famous occasion when they all conspired to pour a tin of white gloss paint over the roof, windscreen and bonnet of a neighbour's dark green car. At first they pretended they had not done it, a line that was hard to sustain for long because their hands were covered with white paint. When they eventually confessed, they said that they had done it because they did not like the colour of the car. Helen and I were furious, and offered to pay for the damage. But the car's owner was surprisingly relaxed and refused, saying it was an old banger that needed replacing anyway. Growing up fast, Gemma seemed to get into trouble easily, but it was always difficult to remain angry for long. One look from her big brown eyes or the beginnings of a grin on her lips would melt the hardest heart. It was impossible not to love her.

Gemma and Richenda were typical sisters, loving and hating each other in equal measure. They played all the usual games with each other when they were small – mummies and daddies, doctors and nurses, goodies and baddies. Being the elder and in some ways the more vulnerable, Richenda often used to come off worst when they quarrelled. Richenda's black hair grew very long down her back, and Gemma used to grab hold of it and pull hard. Richenda would pretend to cry so that Gemma would stop to give her a comforting cuddle. But then, when Richenda started laughing at her, Gemma would tug her hair even harder until she really cried. Gemma also used to hide Richenda's school things deliberately and then help her look for them. It was not until Richenda was close to tears with frustration that Gemma would make out that she had found them. Richenda was always telling Gemma secrets, which her would-be confidante would immediately tell the world. This used to make Richenda angry – while Gemma just laughed.

I have particularly fond memories of the first few Christmases we all spent together. Richenda soon began to realise that Santa Claus was a trick played on children by adults, but Gemma was an absolute believer. On Christmas Eve, after they had both been bathed, we put out food and drink for Santa. In the morning, I was sometimes more excited than they were. I used to wake early and make a cup of tea for Steven and myself. As soon as the children woke up they would come and stand at the top of their stairs in their pyjamas, trying desperately to peer down into the living room. When we went down and opened the door, they would both leap around with excitement. 'He's been! He's been!' Gemma would shout and Richenda, temporarily forgetting her scepticism, would join in. After the presents were opened and the resulting mess tidied up, we usually went round to Tina's and spent the rest of the day with her family and our dad. Gemma and Bianca would dance around together in delight, showing each other their presents, joy shining in their eyes.

Throughout the year, of course, we kept visiting the beaches, especially St Bees. Sometimes Steven used to go on his own with the children, and sometimes we all went. But since the beach contamination incident towards the end of my second pregnancy I had found myself less keen to go. I started to feel, without thinking very deeply about it, that there was something vaguely wrong with the place. I sometimes just sat in the car, faintly uneasy, while the others went and played. Gemma had no such hesitation and quickly came to adore the beach, often demanding to go there. She was particularly fond of the swing park nearby and, like any young child, she found the sand and the salt water fascinating. In her first few summers she would stagger around with hardly any clothes on, burying her hands and feet in the sand, splashing in the pools, grinning madly to herself. Sometimes she would roll around on the ground or suddenly sit down up to her chest in water. Like every toddler, she would sometimes cram handfuls of sand into her mouth.

One day towards the end of July 1987, when Gemma was three years eight months old, she was being looked after by Iris, Tina's mother-in-law. It was a blazing hot summer's day, so she decided to take Gemma, along with Richenda, Nikki and Bianca, to St Bees beach. The other three children tore off their tee-shirts and raced around the sand in shorts, shouting, screaming and having fun. Gemma, however, just sat still, looking disconsolate. Despite the efforts of Iris and the other children to interest her in their games, she seemed disinclined to do anything – she was unnaturally lethargic and uncharacteristically sad. Iris wondered whether she might be a little anaemic and in need of some iron. She looked even paler than usual that day and complained that she was tired and constantly thirsty. Although the temperature must have been in the high seventies Fahrenheit, Gemma remained fully clothed. She sat hunched up, hugging her knees and feeling sorry for herself. 'I'm cold,' she kept saying. 'I'm cold.'

Chapter 2

The Disease That Dare Not Speak Its Name

It was an ordinary English summer's day – a little cloudy, but with no rain or wind. The date has always stuck in my mind: Friday, 31 July 1987. I woke up late, at about quarter-past eight, with a sudden realisation that I had to get Gemma to the doctor's by half-past nine. That meant panic stations. With barely enough time to get up and out, I had to rush around the kitchen getting Gemma's breakfast. As I did so, I found myself wondering whether she really did need to go for a check-up. Personally, I did not think that there was anything wrong with her. I had only made the appointment because – after that hot day on the beach – Iris had suggested that Gemma might need a tonic.

Leaving Gemma in her nightie munching cornflakes in front of the television, I dashed upstairs to try and find us both some suitable clothes. Her bedroom, as always, looked immaculate until I opened the first drawer, which was stuffed with leaking pens, screwed-up balls of paper, damaged clothes and old shoes. Gemma was very partial to pretty clothes and had a knack of persuading grown-ups to buy them for her. She was obsessed with smart shoes, especially shiny, patent leather ones. 'Look at the state of these drawers,' I shouted angrily down the stairs. 'I'm never buying you anything nice again, you only ruin it.'

Perhaps sensing that I was particularly bad-tempered that morning, she ignored me. I eventually managed to find her a clean, but creased, fleecy pink summer dress, a pair of white knickers with pink dots and a white vest with a pink rim. I pulled some jeans and an old white tee-shirt on myself and ran back down the stairs. After

I had shouted at her again, she put on the vest and pants without taking her eyes off the television. But when she saw the dress, she threw a minor tantrum: 'I'm not wearing that. It's horrible and it needs ironing.'

We did not have time for such niceties. I picked her up, sat her on my knee and dragged the dress over her head. She was not being particularly bad, but I was very agitated. We seemed to be heading for a major argument – the kind that always erupted when we were in a hurry. When I threatened to give her a good smack, she put on a pout and some crocodile tears appeared. 'I'm going to tell Dad what you said,' she shouted.

'Tell him. He'll probably give you a good hiding himself,' I replied, knowing in reality that Steven would never hit her. She knew this too, so there was not really any point in threatening her.

'I don't care,' she said, turning away in a sulk. Putting on her socks, I tried a different tactic: bribery instead of confrontation. I told her that if we were quick we might be able to call in at her Aunt Tina's to see her best friend Bianca on the way to the doctor's. Her demeanour immediately changed, and she urged me to hurry up and find her sandals. Then I found a hairbrush and a blue hair-bobble, sat on the edge of the sofa and asked her to come and kneel down by me.

'Let me wear my hair down today. It kills me when you put it up,' Gemma pleaded. But I put it up in a pony-tail. Then I carried her up the stairs and washed her face so fast that she did not have time to complain. On the way back down she told me that we had forgotten to brush her teeth, so I said we would have to do it when we got back. I put on her little white summer jacket and we headed for the door. Before we got out, she reminded me that I had forgotten to turn off the television. I went back and realised I had also left my purse and keys on the sofa. I gave Gemma my purse to hold and – at last – we set off for the centre of Cleator Moor.

After walking for about two or three minutes, Gemma started to complain that her legs were hurting and said she wanted to be carried. I grabbed hold of her hand and literally dragged her up the hill: I was not going to spoil her by carrying her. She fell into another sulk, which she abandoned a little further on when we came to a wall that she loved to clamber along. I lifted her up and held her hand as she ran and jumped along the top. At the end, as always, she held both my hands tightly and leaped off, laughing.

Almost as soon as we started walking again, Gemma complained about her legs. Like any mother, I pointed out that her legs had miraculously stopped hurting while she was playing on the wall. Approaching Tina's house, I suggested that we would probably not now have enough time to pop in, but Gemma would not hear of it. She ran ahead, knocked on the door and shouted 'Bianca!' through the letterbox. Tina, with Bianca still in her nightie, invited us in. We still had twenty-five minutes to get to the doctor's. I sat down gratefully for the morning's first cup of tea while Gemma tucked into a second bowl of cereal. She told Bianca that she was going to the doctor's to play with the toys. Bianca asked me if she could come too, so I told her that we would stop by afterwards. Tina talked excitedly about the seven acres of land she had just bought with the idea of designing and building her own bungalow.

I was dreading arriving at Dr Sydney's surgery, because the waiting room was usually very full and Gemma would get easily bored. Strangely, that morning it was empty. The receptionist asked Gemma's name and sent us straight through. We knocked on the doctor's door and he shouted for us to come in. He said hello to Gemma, then me, and asked us to sit down. I lifted Gemma on to my knee. She, like the curious child that she was, started eyeing everything in the surgery.

Dr Sydney sat back, and asked why we had come. I told him what had happened on the beach and what Iris had said. I felt a little silly because it sounded so insignificant. He asked what I thought. While he started to give Gemma's eyes, ears and throat a routine check, I described how she always seemed tired and complained of aching legs after walking a short distance. I told him about her raging thirst: no matter how much fluid I gave her, she always wanted more. I talked about how she ate and ate all the time, how her stomach was often swollen like a balloon, and how her legs were often covered with bruises. I thought all these things were irrelevant or unsurprising for a child of her age, but when you are at the doctor's you are meant to mention everything. I had no idea that I was describing the symptoms which led directly to her diagnosis.

Dr Sydney lifted Gemma on to the examination couch and asked if he could look at her tummy. She said no. He managed to persuade her by promising that he would not hurt her. But when he asked her to pull up her dress, she got embarrassed. She did not like anybody looking at her knickers. He pressed her stomach, asking if it hurt. She just lay there and shook her head, unwilling to speak to the man who had seen her underwear.

Asking Gemma to stay on the bed, he disappeared out of the room. She asked me if she could get up and pull her dress down. I told her to lie still, which, rather unwillingly, she did. She gave me a fiercely disapproving look when Dr Sydney returned almost immediately with a colleague. That meant that two men would see her knickers. I held her hand while they both examined her stomach. Neither of them said anything, but the second doctor nodded at Dr Sydney and then left the room. I was starting to get anxious. Only something potentially serious would need a second opinion.

Gemma jumped off the bed and begged for a drink of 'murk'. Dr Sydney was mystified until I explained that she meant milk. He buzzed through to the receptionist and asked her to bring through a glass. This struck me as unusual, and fanned the flames of fear that were beginning to burn across my brain. Remembering that Steven's father had suffered from angina, I asked: 'Is it her heart?'

'No,' he replied, 'but there is a lot they can do these days.'

'Is it her kidneys?'

'No.'

'Is she anaemic?'

'Yes.' For a moment I felt relieved. It sounded such a simple, common, curable condition. But then came his refrain: 'There's a lot they can do these days.'

It was getting difficult to escape the feeling that something serious could be wrong with Gemma. Deep down I had a strong suspicion what it might be, as there had been quite a few cases in our area and some publicity about them recently. It was a disease that Tina, Steven and I had talked about, wondering whether we should worry about our children. But I was not sure, and felt very ignorant. Almost consciously, I decided to avoid thinking about it. I formed this irrational notion that refusing to name the disease might make it go away.

By this time Gemma was getting impatient. She was wandering around the surgery, looking at pictures and fiddling with a set of scales. The doctor told me I would have to take her to Whitehaven Hospital for a blood test. I asked when the appointment would be. 'No, no, you misunderstand me,' he said. 'She must go now. I will call you an ambulance.'

There was no need, I said, suggesting that I would ring my sister to take us instead. On the telephone Tina asked what was the matter with Gemma. I told her that the doctor did not know, but that it was something to do with her thirst, her stomach, her bruises and her constant tiredness. The aim of the blood test was to find out. Tina arrived in minutes. Seeing the fear in my eyes, she sought to reassure me that it was not what I thought. The doctor gave us a sealed letter for the hospital consultant. I remember telling him that I wished I had never come to his surgery. He made me promise to go to the hospital, which I did, and then thanked him.

'It's amazing what they can do these days,' he said.

Gemma was happy when she got into Tina's car because Bianca was sitting in the back. I sat in the front and asked Tina if I should cry. She told me again that it was probably nothing serious, and certainly not what I feared. Before going to the hospital we went back to Tina's to try and contact Steven at work in Sellafield. I telephoned his employers and asked them to pass him an urgent message: 'Gemma has to go to hospital for a blood test.' They were very sympathetic and Steven rang back within a few minutes. I told him what had happened at the surgery. Like Tina, he knew instinctively what I was worried about, but told me not to think the worst. He said he would come straight home.

While we were waiting for him, Gemma played happily with

Bianca, who was still in her nightie. Tina ran around getting her dressed, just like I had done with Gemma earlier, and telephoned Iris to come in and look after her. I drank a cup of tea, smoked a cigarette and tried to keep calm. Gemma did not understand what was happening, and I thought it best not to worry her by explaining anything. When Steven arrived, she was reluctant to put her coat on to go back out because she was enjoying playing so much. She asked whether Bianca could come with us. I told her that Bianca had to stay at home, but then when we came back they could play together all day if they wanted to. I did not really believe what I was saying.

Bianca burst into tears, insisting that she wanted to come. Iris, who had just arrived, swept her away upstairs while we got into Steven's car. It was the best car we had ever owned – a metallic pink Stanza – and Gemma was very proud of it. She and Tina sat in the back, with Steven and me in the front. 'Why are we going to the hospital, Mam?' she asked as we set off. 'I feel all right.'

'They want to make sure that you are OK, Gemma. It won't take long.'

It was mid-morning when we arrived at the hospital, where it was surprisingly easy to get parked. Just like hospital visitors, the four of us made our way to the children's ward. It was very quiet and there were no nurses to be seen anywhere. A little at a loss, we walked down a long corridor with lots of closed doors on either side. Steven remarked how he hated the smell of hospitals – all disinfectant and institutional food. A nurse finally emerged from one of the many side rooms and asked who we were looking for. I said we were there to see the consultant paediatrician. She told us to wait while she tried to find him.

She seemed to be gone for ages but then finally reappeared at the end of the corridor with a sophisticated-looking man. Instead of a white coat, he was wearing a dark suit, white shirt and bow tie. He introduced himself to us as Dr Roberts, and I explained who we were and handed him the letter from Dr Sydney. He said he had to see someone before us and left us sitting outside his door. Gemma started getting bored. She picked up a book from a shelf, and Tina started to read it to her. We seemed to wait hours, but I suppose it was only minutes. We hardly spoke to each other, except to ask the time. All the while it felt as if we were trapped in a time warp.

At last we were called in. Steven took Gemma's hand, all four of us stood up and moved towards the door. But Dr Roberts asked Tina to wait outside, which made her feel left out. He assured her that we would not be long. His office was small and rectangular, with a window at the far end. He sat behind a desk faced by two plastic chairs, surrounded by mountains of paperwork. 'Right, let's take a look at you, Emma,' he said.

'Gemma,' she corrected him, from her perch on Steven's knee. Dr Roberts examined her eyes and nodded to himself. He felt her stomach and muttered to himself. Then he said that he wanted to take a quick blood test to make sure.

'To make sure of what?' I queried, but he did not answer. He went out of the door to the adjoining treatment room and returned with a test tube and a sharp blade. I realised what this was for, but Gemma did not. Steven could not stand the sight of blood, so I beckoned her to me. I held her hand firmly, but before the blade had even touched her she started to scream and struggle. Dr Roberts managed to jab her thumb and was desperately trying to squeeze some blood into his test tube, but it was dripping everywhere. I tried to calm her down by suggesting that if she kept still it would be over much quicker. Although she was not listening, I kept talking. Dr Roberts was trying to speak to her too, and we both became fraught. Rather briskly, I thought, he told me to be quiet so that he could do the talking.

That made me mad. I pulled Gemma's hand away and she ran back sobbing to Steven. I was shaking. I demanded to know the whereabouts of the haematology department so that the blood sample could be taken there. Dr Roberts told me, but suggested the department's staff would not be able to do it any less painfully. I glanced back as we walked out of his room. 'We'll see,' I said.

In the corridor, I explained to Tina what had happened. Steven was carrying Gemma, who was clutching her thumb tightly and crying. We took a lift to the third floor and walked down a long, dark corridor through endless sets of double fire doors before we reached the haematology department. I walked past a row of hard plastic chairs and knocked loudly on the door, which was opened by a bearded man in a white lab coat. He was expecting us, and asked us to go into the next room and have a seat. He called his female assistant, Lyn, into the room. He knelt down next to Gemma, who was sitting on my knee, and told her that good children got to see the lovely surprise that was hidden in his drawer. Lyn took hold of Gemma's hand and promised her that it would not hurt a lot if she concentrated her imagination on the contents of the drawer. She then pricked Gemma's thumb.

Gemma still screamed, but stopped almost straightaway. Lyn gently squeezed her thumb and smeared a little blood on to three glass slides. Then she said it was all over and led her by the hand to the drawer. Gemma was holding a piece of cotton wool over the end of her thumb. I asked the man in the white coat what they were looking for in her blood. Was it to see if she was anaemic? He said it was, but I knew that was not all. I looked at Steven and he sighed.

'Look, Mam, look what I've got.' Gemma came running excitedly back clutching two sherbet dips, one for her and one for Bianca. She had asked for extra packets for half a dozen of her other friends and relations, but Lyn had insisted that that would leave none for other brave children who came for blood tests. Somewhat reluctantly, Gemma surrendered Bianca's dip to Tina. The man in the white coat told us to go back to the children's ward to see Dr Roberts again. Gemma objected, but calmed down after we opened her sherbet for her.

On the way back Gemma smelt a food trolley trundling past and said she was hungry. When we arrived at Dr Roberts' room, we had to sit and wait in a corridor surrounded by children playing with toys. Gemma found a tricycle that was far too small for her and rode it round and round in tight circles at breakneck speed. I stared at her and thought she could not be seriously ill. I tried to believe that she was simply anaemic. I tried to convince myself that she did not have the unnamed disease. Just thinking the word would be tempting fate.

After nearly half an hour, Dr Roberts called us back into his surgery, again asking Tina to wait outside. We walked in, and Gemma sat on Steven's knee with her head on his chest. She felt secure close to her Dad. She did not want the doctor with the bow tie to come near in case he hurt her again. Dr Roberts asked Gemma whether he could look into her eyes again. She looked questioningly at Steven, who nodded and said it would be all right. Dr Roberts peered into her eyes until she started getting restless. 'Good heavens, Gemma, you're very anaemic, aren't you?' he said, prompting Steven and me to exchange glances again.

Dr Roberts asked Gemma if she would like to go and play outside in the corridor with her aunt. Opening the door, he suggested to Tina that she ask the nurse for a spare dinner if Gemma was hungry. Gemma rushed out and jumped into Tina's arms. 'Please,' she said in a baby voice, looking for all the world as if she was a poor, starving wretch who had not eaten for weeks. Tina assented with a smile, and I could hear them laughing as they walked off down the corridor. She cannot be ill, I thought again.

Dr Roberts came back into the room and closed the door as if he was closing a chapter of my life. What he was about to tell us would change everything for ever. He walked over to his desk and turned quickly to face Steven and me. It was as if thinking about what he had to say might prevent him from saying it. He blurted out the words.

'I'm sorry to have to tell you, but Gemma has got leukaemia.'

Chapter 3

White Blood

The words the doctor had spoken hung menacingly in the air. I was staring fixedly at the door. I remember the white paint was chipped and dirty. Numbness was the first feeling, followed immediately by disbelief. Then, inside me bubbled up a powerful cauldron of fear, despair and anger all at once. After that came a host of anxieties. How would I tell Tina? How would we tell Gemma and Richenda? How would they react? What did leukaemia mean? Why had Gemma caught it? I looked at Steven as if to say 'I told you so.' He dropped his head and clutched his body as though he had just been fisted hard in the stomach. He lifted his head again and looked at me, appealing for a reason. I did not know what to say.

After a pause, I asked Dr Roberts how long Gemma had left, although I did not really want to know the answer. He said that he was sorry, but it was impossible to tell at that moment. She needed to attend a specialist clinic for further tests and treatment as soon as possible. We would have to drive over to the Royal Victoria Infirmary in Newcastle that afternoon, although he warned us not to drive too fast. A few hours, he said, was not going to make any difference. He suggested we prepare for a stay of several days. He was going to give us a letter of introduction and draw us a map, but he was unable to answer any more questions.

Shell-shocked, Steven and I walked out into the corridor. Tina was not in sight, but we could see Gemma. She had already scoffed her lunch and was cycling round in circles again on the tiny tricycle. I looked at her and thought: 'You're going to die.' I somehow got it into my head that she was going to drop at any second. I told

Dr Roberts I was worried about telling Tina. He asked a nurse to take me to the parents' room for some privacy, promising to send Tina after me. I left Steven keeping an eye on Gemma, still going round and round, giggling.

The parents' room was small, with a television, a table and plastic armchairs lining the walls. There were ashtrays all over the place and a public payphone in a cubicle. I could hear someone talking on the phone, but the nurse asked whoever it was to leave for a few minutes. I sat down and the nurse sat next to me on the edge of her seat, stretching out to hold my hand. Through a small window in the door I caught a glimpse of Tina's face. As she came in, the nurse let go of my hand. So far I had not cried.

'What's wrong? What's the doctor said?' Tina asked, glancing at me and the nurse, who turned away. Sensing something, her eyes began to fill.

'She's got leukaemia,' I said flatly.

'Who has?' she asked without thinking.

'Gemma – she's got leukaemia.'

Tina ran out of the room and back in again screaming: 'No, no, not that! Not that!' I could control myself no longer and broke down. We cried together, hugged each other and talked for a while, searching for consolation. When we had calmed down a little, I told her that we had to go to Newcastle that day for more tests. We did not know much about leukaemia, but we did know that it could be fatal. Tina and I were both obsessed with the same inescapable thought: 'Gemma's got cancer. She's going to die.'

I looked at the telephone. We were going to have to let people know, like our dad, who was working at Sellafield for a contractor. We knew the company's name, but not the number. Tina found 50p and we squeezed into the tiny booth. Directory Enquiries could not find the number, so Tina dialled the operator and explained the problem. She tried to keep calm, but the tears suddenly started rolling again. 'We're in the hospital and my niece has just been diagnosed as having leukaemia. We have to get in touch with our dad straightaway.'

'Calm down, love,' said the operator, clearly moved. 'I'll see what

I can do.' Tina and I stood huddled together, arms around each other, shouting our dad's name and his company down the phone. The operator must have thought that we were crazy, but she got us through. We left a message asking Dad to come home urgently.

Then Steven walked in, having left Gemma playing happily with a nurse. He looked pale. I told him to phone his parents, reminding him to be tactful.

'Hello Mum, it's Steven. We're at the hospital . . . Gemma's got leukaemia.'

The phone went suddenly quiet, and then Steven's dad came on to ask why his mum had nearly passed out. Steven repeated the news, and said he was sorry for being so blunt. He promised we would go and see them as soon as we could.

The door to the parents' room opened again and Diane, a good friend who lived nearby, was standing there. She had been told we were at the hospital and had come down straightaway. When she asked me what the matter was, sobs again started to make my body shake, preventing me from answering. Diane started to cry before Tina had finished explaining what had happened. 'But she looks fine. I've just passed her playing and laughing in the corridor,' Diane sobbed in disbelief. 'She told me where you were.'

After a while, when we had all recovered, we walked back to where Gemma was playing. She bounded up to Diane, waving her hand. 'Look at my thumb – they took some blood out.'

'Did it hurt?' asked Diane, trying to hide her sadness. Gemma said emphatically that it did, and returned to the tricycle. We told her we had to go home now. As we walked out of the ward, Dr Roberts and the nurses all wished us good luck.

At home Steven disappeared straight up the stairs on his own. I let him be because I knew what he was doing: he was shedding his tears in private. I hurriedly packed some clothes in a suitcase and we all walked back out to the car. For some reason I felt as if hundreds of eyes were peering at us through curtains along the street, but it was just my imagination.

'Where are we going?' asked Gemma, mildly confused by the morning's events. Although we had told her nothing, she instinctively realised that she had become the centre of attention. She sensed that adults were acting differently towards her, showing her more affection. She was enjoying it immensely. I explained that we were going first to Steven's parents, who lived a few miles away.

When we arrived there, arms were flung around us. As well as Steven's parents, his brother and his wife had left work to come and see us. I pleaded with Steven's mum not to cry in front of Gemma, trying to stem my own tears at the same time. Steven took Gemma off to play and I explained as best I could what was happening. They wished us the best of luck and told us to telephone if we needed anything.

Then we drove back to Tina's, where my father was waiting. All I wanted him to do was to put his arms around me and hold me. But there was too much going on and he did not. While we were having a cup of tea, Richenda came in with Helen's daughter, Kerry. She had no idea about what had been happening. She told me that Kerry was going away camping for the weekend with the play scheme, and begged to be allowed to go too.

I agreed almost at once, thinking it might be helpful to keep her away from unfolding events. She was thrilled and ran off excitedly to play with Kerry. By then it was three o'clock in the afternoon and we still had a two-and-a-half-hour drive to Newcastle, followed by God-only-knew-what at the hospital. Steven pointed out that we had to get moving, and so, with Tina and her husband, Russell, we set off. Just past Carlisle Gemma decided that she had to go to the toilet. I told her not to panic and tried to distract her. We were all treating her like a queen as if she only had a couple of hours to live. It was an unbelievable feeling. After four miles we found a public toilet.

When we arrived at the Royal Victoria Infirmary, Gemma took hold of Tina and Russell's hands and skipped inside. It seemed like a huge, crumbling old place. We asked directions to Ward 16 South, and Gemma, still skipping, led the way. She was very happy, as if she was going on holiday. At first the ward looked surprisingly small, as we walked past a treatment room, a kitchen and two empty beds to reach the nurses' office. 'This can't be Gemma,' a nurse said. 'We were expecting her to be carried in. She has a very low blood count.' I did not really know what she meant, but I assured her it was.

We walked through the rest of the ward to the play area to wait for the doctor. We passed seven beds, three on one side, four on another, all containing young children. They had tubes coming out of their bodies into machines, and bags of blood hanging from stands. Some were asleep and some were vomiting into bowls, although they still managed to smile as we passed. Several were completely bald. Parents were sitting next to some of the beds, looking exhausted.

We sat in the tiny play area, facing the ward and saying nothing. I kept wondering if Gemma was going to have to suffer and lose her hair like these children. But, busy playing with a child's computer, she just ignored them. I felt as if something inside was about to snap. I suggested to Tina that we should just walk out of the ward and buy ourselves private medical care somewhere else. Anything would be better than this. She reminded me that there was no way we could afford to. After about half an hour, a nurse came with an admission form for us to fill in. A little angrily, I complained about how long we had been waiting. Then almost immediately a tall, slim, besuited man, wearing glasses and greying at the temples, introduced himself as Dr Alan Craft. In the midst of the play area, he began to examine Gemma.

His attitude towards her was superb, carefully explaining what he was doing in language that she could understand. Towards us he acted differently, as though his job was to treat the patient and not the parents. I knew this was right, but at that moment we were hurting more than Gemma and would have appreciated a little more sympathy. He told us there were three or four different types of leukaemia, all of which required different types of treatment. More tests would be necessary to establish which type Gemma had. The hospital would find her a bed so she could stay the night.

Tina and Russell decided they had to go back home to their own children. I promised to phone them later, but then felt suddenly jealous that they could just walk out of my nightmare. I know it was silly but I begged them to stay, saying how scared I was. But

Steven assured them that we would be all right and firmly sent them off. They kissed Gemma goodbye and strode quickly out of sight down the ward. It was not until later that I learned that Tina had cried all the way home, wanting to turn back. She later wrote:

> The day Gemma was diagnosed was like being told she was going to explode at any minute like a time bomb. If someone had said that cutting my arms off would have made her better, I would gladly have given them. Part of me died that day . . . Gemma was my niece and my daughter's best friend. When she was diagnosed I felt guilty that my daughter was all right, and then guilty for even thinking it.

Gemma's hospital bed had curtains for a little privacy, and a single chair. It was next to a door marked 'Sluice', through which used bedpans and vomit bowls were carried. Every time the door opened, an unpleasant smell wafted out.

While Gemma was getting ready for bed, a young man approached me. 'Hi, my name's Paul. I'm a parent here too. I was just wondering if you would like a cup of tea or coffee?' he smiled.

I don't know why, but I started to sob again. 'I'm sorry,' I said, 'but you're the first person to ask. We've been on the go since this morning. I'd love a cup. I don't suppose there is anywhere we could go and have a cigarette, is there?'

We found a nurse to look after Gemma, who told us not to be long, then Steven and I followed Paul through an unmarked door to a long room full of vending machines and easy chairs. As we drank, Paul told us that his eight-month baby boy was starting treatment on a tumour in his stomach the following day. I could not believe how happy he sounded, knowing that the treatment would probably make his child very ill. 'It's my baby's only hope, his only chance of life,' he explained.

Paul returned to the ward, leaving Steven and me alone for the first time that day. 'I don't know whether I can handle this,' I said. 'I wish we hadn't gone to the doctor's this morning – then we wouldn't be here now and we would still be a normal family. It's all my fault.'

'We have to be strong for Gemma's sake,' Steven said quietly, trying to comfort me. 'She's a strong girl, Susan, a fighter.'

'I know, but all I keep thinking is that she's going to die.'

We walked slowly back to the ward, preparing again to hide our fear from Gemma. 'Hi, Mam,' Gemma shouted, 'Guess what? I've got leukaemia.' I was shocked to hear her say this and looked at the nurse. She told me not to be surprised, and explained that the ward's policy was to be as honest as possible with both parents and children. Telling lies, or not correcting misconceptions, made things much harder in the future. Gemma now knew the word 'leukaemia', although she did not really understand what it meant. But we could all talk more freely in front of her, without whispering or subterfuge.

As we tried to settle Gemma down for the night – a difficult task at the best of times – she got a brush and hand-mirror out of her bedside drawer. I had not seen them before, and she told me that Tina had left them for her. Holding the mirror in front of her but not looking at it, she starting slowly and inexpertly trying to brush her long brown hair. Acutely conscious of the stares from the surrounding children – with hardly a strand of hair between them – I wanted to snatch the brush from her hand. I wondered whether her hair would soon be falling out in lumps.

After we had assured Gemma that one of us would stay with her through the night, she eventually drifted off to sleep. For her it had been an exciting as well as tiring day. We visited the parents' bedroom, which was far away along corridors and up stairs at the other end of the hospital. It was quite spacious, with its own washing and cooking facilities, but it only had a single bed. Steven and I argued about who was going to sleep in it and who was going to stay with Gemma.

On the way back to the ward, we stopped to phone Tina. I apologised for making a fuss when she left, and she apologised for having to leave. I made sure Richenda was all right and then the phone ran out of money. As I replaced the receiver, I was crying again. Steven put his arm around me, urging me to think positive. But my thoughts were still all irretrievably negative.

All the children were asleep when we got back. We sat next to Gemma, me on her bed and Steven on the only chair, and stared at her sleeping until it grew late. Steven eventually went off reluctantly to the parents' room to try and get some sleep. I settled down in the chair with my feet on Gemma's bed. I drifted in and out of sleep, and at some point someone put a blanket over me. Around three in the morning, I was woken up by the night nurse gently tapping me. She suggested I would be more comfortable if I climbed in with Gemma. I agreed and lay down beside her. Gemma turned and snuggled up to me.

The ward started to wake up at around half-past six. Small children cried, machines bleeped and people walked up and down. It was Saturday morning. When Gemma woke up I was trying to make a cup of tea in the kitchenette nearby. She shouted for me, and I appeared from round the corner offering her a drink. She needed the toilet urgently and I had to ask someone where it was.

After I had helped Gemma dress, Steven appeared. 'Hiya, Gem, you OK?' he said.

'No,' she grinned, pointing at me, 'she's terrible to sleep with.' Just like her father, I thought.

After breakfast, Dr Craft arrived. We accompanied him and a nurse to a treatment room, where he told Gemma that he wanted to take some blood from her. Remembering what had happened previously, she objected. After a few tears and screams, a butterfly needle was inserted into her hand. The blood was drawn off and the needle was left in her hand, which was then bandaged. Dr Craft told us he would have a word with us in private later when the results of the tests came through. Steven looked at me. We still knew virtually nothing about Gemma's condition.

Back in the ward, Gemma played with other children in the play area as we waited. I felt as if we had been there for weeks, instead of eighteen hours. As the day dragged on, I found myself getting tense and angry. There was no privacy and my emotions were all over the place. I kept wanting to cry, but had to stop myself because I was always in the presence of children and parents. The hospital offered us a parents' room with twin beds, and to pass the time we took Gemma to see it. On the way she started complaining that her legs were sore, so Steven had to carry her.

'This is nice,' said Gemma, with a hint of jealousy in her voice when we got there. 'Why can't I stay here with you and Dad?'

I told her that she had to stay in the ward because the doctors and nurses had to keep an eye on her. But she insisted that she was not ill. She helped me make tea, in the process opening every drawer and cupboard in the place. We found two teabags and some milk, but no sugar. I pointed out that Steven would not drink it without sugar. 'Never mind,' grinned Gemma. 'Me and you can have a cup and Dad can have one later.'

After a while Gemma started to get bored and we enticed her back to the ward with the prospect of the dinner trolley. There a nurse told us that Dr Craft was now ready to see us. After she had shown us the way, she took Gemma off to play. Dr Craft was sitting in what seemed like an attic room. On the table in front of him there was a manilla folder with Gemma's name on it. He opened it and began.

He told us that leukaemia was a disease that progressively damaged the balance of life-giving cells in the blood. It infected the bone marrow, where blood cells are produced, often leading to an excess of white blood cells which eventually overwhelm the body. The word leukaemia comes from the Greek, meaning 'white blood'.

There were several different forms of the disease, some relatively common and others relatively rare. Gemma's condition was one of the rarest and was known as chronic myeloid leukaemia. Given her condition, she seemed surprising healthy, so there was probably no need at the moment for a blood transfusion. But her treatment should begin with an initial course of mild chemotherapy with the aim of restoring the balance of her blood cells. Ultimately she would need a bone marrow transplant. Dr Craft said he realised that this would all sound alien to us, but promised he would try and help us understand.

Until then Steven and I had just been listening without saying anything. When I asked the first question, my voice was hoarse. I wanted to know exactly how rare Gemma's type of leukaemia was. Dr Craft replied that, although it was quite common amongst elderly people, it was extremely rare in children. He would expect to see no more than two or three child cases a year from throughout the country. Unfortunately, because it was so rare doctors knew less about it than they did about other forms of leukaemia. Elderly sufferers often died of old age before the disease had had time to take hold. It was known, however, that chronic myeloid leukaemia did respond to oral chemotherapy, using a drug know as busulphan. It was not a cure, but it did seem to hold the disease at bay for a while.

'How long is a while?' asked Steven.

Dr Craft explained that the drug acted to suppress the bone marrow's over-production of white blood cells which were making Gemma look anaemic and feel tired. It would probably make her feel much better, as it had other leukaemia victims in the past, although it could also inflict damage on the bone marrow. There was no way of predicting how long it would remain effective. It should work for up to three years; with luck it could stretch to ten, but no one could be certain.

His explanation seemed to me to be suggesting that Gemma could only have three years left to live. He said that was not necessarily the case, as the eventual outcome could depend on giving Gemma someone else's bone marrow to replace her own – a bone marrow transplant. This was a very unpleasant operation, which required a donor whose bone marrow perfectly matched that of the patient. The best hope for such a donor was a member of the immediate family, particularly a brother or sister, but even then only one in four produced perfectly matching marrow. Steven, Richenda and I could all be tested to see if our bone marrow might be suitable.

But, Dr Craft emphasised, those were decisions for the future. In the meantime, he would start Gemma straightaway on a course of busulphan, which should enable her to lead a relatively normal life. Because it would only be a small dose, it would not cause some of the more unpleasant side-effects of chemotherapy, like sickness and hair loss. It would also be necessary for Gemma to have an operation in the next couple of days to extract a small sample of her bone marrow in order to assess precisely how the leukaemia was progressing. After that, Dr Craft said, she could go home.

As I listened, all kinds of thoughts tumbled through my head. The doctor had just told us that our daughter had as little as three years to live and yet we were all going home in a few days. This did not seem to make sense to me. Much of what he had said I only dimly understood. There were too many alien concepts, too many unfamiliar words, too many scary scenarios. It was impossible to take in the enormity of what we were being told, let alone the details. Questions flooded to the front of my mind. What caused leukaemia? Was it something we had done as parents? Was it because we smoked? Was it because we fed Gemma the wrong food? Was it because I smacked her too hard when she had been naughty? Was it anything to do with where we lived or worked? Could it be connected to Sellafield?

Dr Craft shook his head. He stressed that the cause was unknown, and that a great deal of research was being conducted to try and discover it. There could be a whole series of factors, either individually or together, which helped trigger it. They included radiation, toxic chemicals, tobacco, drugs and viruses. The only factor on which there was hard evidence of a link to chronic myeloid leukaemia was radiation, but that did not necessarily implicate Sellafield. The doctor stressed that the number of people who recovered from leukaemia was increasing. There was no point in blaming ourselves or our environment, he said. We had to concentrate on Gemma. She was the one who needed our help now.

Steven sat back in his chair, with his hands on his head as if he was trying to wipe away the pain. Dr Craft made clear that the consultation was coming to an end. He promised to keep us informed as we went along, and we thanked him. As we turned to go, I asked him again for the name of Gemma's leukaemia and he repeated it.

Instead of going straight back to the ward, Steven and I went for a coffee on our own. He fumbled for change at the vending machine while I stared out of the window, without focusing, at the back wall of the hospital.

'Are you all right?' Steven asked nervously.

'Are you?' I responded.

He shrugged his shoulders.

'Three years,' I said. 'Three years.'

Steven again urged me not to be so pessimistic. He said it was much too soon to give up hope. There was always the possibility of a transplant. I pointed out that we had to find a match, but then started talking about all the people whom we knew who could be tested to see if their bone marrow was the same as Gemma's. There had to be some hope.

Back in the ward, Gemma, pleased as Punch, told us that she had been helping to dish out the dinners. Another parent told me Tina had phoned. Gemma's nurse asked if we had understood what Dr Craft had told us. I said that I thought we had. Gemma was suffering from a rare form of leukaemia that was incurable unless she was given a bone marrow transplant. Without a successful transplant, her life expectancy was between three and ten years. That was the blunt truth, the nurse agreed, but, like Steven, she urged me to cling on to hope. As long as Gemma was alive and enjoying life, there was something to fight for. Feeling foolish, I said that I kept forgetting the name of Gemma's leukaemia and asked the nurse to write it down on a piece of paper for me.

The nurse showed me the best way of persuading Gemma to swallow her busulphan tablets, which she initially refused to take. When two pills arrived in a plastic cup, they were mixed and crushed in a few drops of Coca Cola. To my amazement, Gemma swallowed them with no objection. The nurse then explained the procedure for the operation to remove the bone marrow sample from Gemma, which Dr Craft had arranged to be performed in two days' time. Gemma would not be allowed to have anything to eat or drink from midnight the night before. She would be put to sleep with gas, and then a needle would be inserted into the middle of her hip bone to draw off bone marrow ('the yellow stuff that you see dogs trying to get out of bones'). Her leg would be stiff for an hour or two after she woke up.

We phoned Tina and Steven's parents again to pass on the latest news. I told Tina not to tell Richenda, so that we could tell her ourselves when we next saw her. She said lots of people had already been asking after Gemma.

We spent the rest of the day trying to keep her happy, which was not always easy cooped up in a small ward with sick children, far away from her friends. We played silly games, did jigsaws and watched the television. At one point Gemma asked if she could stay the night with us in the parents' room because she did not like it on the ward. At the suggestion that this would not be possible, she started crying. I said I would ask the doctors and nurses at bedtime. When I did, we were told that it would be all right as long as we were back on the ward for breakfast.

Gemma was very happy to make her escape, although she was a disaster to sleep with, her arms and legs flailing everywhere in the single bed. The next morning one of the staff told us that the nursing sister had not in fact been pleased that we were away from the ward for the night. The problem, apparently, was not that we were not trusted to look after our own daughter, but that Gemma, once admitted to hospital, was the medical staff's responsibility and they would get the blame if anything went wrong. I responded sourly that it was not up to the hospital staff whether they trusted me or not. I was Gemma's mother and she was first and foremost my responsibility. I then immediately regretted what I had said, and apologised. I promised that Gemma would sleep on the ward that night. My nerves were on edge.

For most of the day we sat around again, trying to keep Gemma amused. Tina called on the ward's Mickey Mouse phone to say she was bringing Richenda, Bianca and Nikki over later on. On one occasion I escaped for coffee and started talking to another parent, called Linda. 'What ward are you on?' she asked.

'16 South,' I said.

'North, don't you mean?'

'No, South. My daughter has leukaemia.' That was the first time

I had told anyone other than family, and it felt strange. She told me that her son was on Ward 16 North across the corridor with asthma. We must have talked for over an hour. On the way back, she turned left into 16 North and I turned right into 16 South: a few steps apart, but a world of difference between.

In the afternoon little Bianca appeared at the ward swing doors, followed closely by her parents, her brother and Richenda. We all decamped to the parents' room, avoiding Richenda's questions about what was wrong with Gemma by asking her about her weekend camping trip. When we got there Steven and I sat down on the bed to explain everything to Richenda while Gemma showed the others how to make tea.

Richenda's reaction, for an eight-year-old, was deeply shocking. 'Gemma's going to die,' she said. 'Everyone dies of leukaemia. My teacher's little girl died of it. So did the little boy who was at my school. Is she going to lose all her hair like the others?'

'No, she's different,' I said.

Gemma popped her head round the corner to correct me. 'I'm not different, I'm special.'

Richenda flashed a smile at her. 'That doesn't mean I can't give you a good hiding.'

While the children played around us, Tina, Russell, Steven and I had our first serious conversation about all that had transpired over the last three days. Tina wondered what kind of fate had chosen Gemma out of the millions of other healthy children in the world. When it was time for them to go, Tina gave Gemma a big kiss. 'Yuk,' said Gemma loudly, wiping her face with her sleeve. For the first time in ages we all laughed.

The next morning when Gemma woke up, she immediately demanded breakfast as usual. We explained that she was not allowed any food because of the bone marrow operation she was having later in the day. She was not overjoyed at this news, but we told her that she could eat as much as she liked afterwards. After Steven and I returned from a snatched cup of coffee, a nurse told us that Gemma had been round all the other parents in the ward begging for a drink. When that failed she had tried to bribe the children by promising them an invitation to her party in exchange for a sip of drink. She also tried to steal an orangeade carton. We had to laugh.

Tina reappeared after a while, which helped keep Gemma's mind off food. Then Gemma was at last wheeled off to the operating theatre, where the men in masks and green overalls frightened her. But they soon had her in their spell when they asked her if she had heard of magic wind. After Steven had smelt it first, Gemma agreed to take deep breaths of magic wind through the anaesthetist's cupped hands. After a short struggle she fell peacefully asleep.

Tina, Steven and I waited outside for a while, but then were told to go back to the ward. Eventually the anaesthetist arrived, carrying Gemma, still asleep, in his arms. We felt a huge sense of relief as he gently laid her on her bed. We were told to wake her up after an hour, but she lashed about, complaining that her hip was sore and that she wanted to go back to sleep. It was not until Steven's family arrived later that she managed to forget the pain. That night she slept soundly, and I escaped for the first time to the parents' room.

The following morning Gemma limped around moaning for a while until she got bored with it. The only marks from the operation were two small holes like a vampire bite in her hip.

After lunch, Dr Craft sought us out and confirmed the diagnosis. It was definitely chronic myeloid leukaemia, and Gemma had probably been suffering from it for the last six to eight months. There were signs that the busulphan tablets were starting to work because her red blood count was slowly improving. A blood transfusion would not be necessary at this stage, but he could not predict precisely when the leukaemia would become acute, although it was likely to be between three and ten years. Dr Craft asked Gemma how she felt, and she said she felt fine. 'I don't see why you can't go home now,' he concluded. 'We'll get the hospital pharmacy to give you a supply of tablets, and if you have any worries you can phone us. We are open twenty-four hours a day.'

A couple of hours later we were all walking out along the corridor with our bags, a letter for our general practitioner and a large bottle of busulphan. We had been warned to keep Gemma away from anyone who had had contact with measles or chicken pox, as she would be unable to fight off the infections. We felt relieved and excited to be heading home. It was like being released from a hideous, nightmarish and unreal prison into the simple comfort of the known and the understood.

As we searched the car park for the car that Tina had left us, I felt almost light-headed. Four days earlier I had walked into my doctor's surgery with a child who just seemed a little off-colour. Now I was leaving with a little girl who, despite her healthy appearance, I knew to be terminally ill. It was almost impossible to accept what had happened, to come to terms with the way all our lives had so radically changed. The main feeling was one of utter bewilderment, coupled with a deep anxiety about the future. But I knew one thing: I needed answers. What had we done to deserve this fate? Why us, I kept wondering, why Gemma?

Chapter 4

The Sellafield Experiment

Since coming to Cumbria in 1974, Sellafield had always been part of my life. Most of my friends and relatives worked there at some point, including Steven, his father, my sister Tina and her husband Russell. Most of the families we came into contact with included Sellafield employees. The plant as an employer was a frequent topic of conversation, a butt of jokes and the cause of all the usual gripes. It dominated the local economy, contributing over a third of the rates bill and employing one in every three workers. Its 7,200 employees have in turn tended to dominate local politics, forming up to a quarter of the local borough's councillors. Sellafield's operator, the government-owned British Nuclear Fuels plc, has also thrown its money about locally, spending £3.5 million on rebuilding Whitehaven town centre and £10 million over ten years on the West Cumbrian Development Agency. It has always had the enthusiastic support of the high-ranking local Labour MP, Dr Jack Cunningham, who in 1986 accepted the chairmanship of a local group of pro-nuclear worthies known as the Friends of Sellafield.

To be honest, though, I never really thought that much about the plant until Gemma was diagnosed with leukaemia. It was only then that all the things I had heard began to resurface in my brain. Stories from Steven and incidental pieces of information I had picked up from others took on new meanings. I thought more about the place, talked to more people about it and found out about its history and its safety record. I tried to learn about nuclear radiation and its possible health effects, and I did not always like what I discovered.

I began to form opinions about nuclear power – opinions that were not always popular with the rest of my family, not to mention the local community.

Ionising, or nuclear, radiation occurs naturally but only in low concentrations. Conventional nuclear power stations, fuelled by uranium mined from the ground, are a means of concentrating natural radioactivity and using it to make electricity for use in homes and industry. Uranium fuel rods are irradiated or 'burnt' in nuclear reactors, and the heat that is produced is used to raise steam to turn turbines – the same as in coal- or oil-fired power stations. The problem is that during this process the uranium is transformed from a mildly radioactive raw material into a messy conglomeration of highly radioactive elements, most of which are as dangerous as they are useless. This mess is known as spent fuel, and its treatment, or reprocessing, is at the root of the environmental problems created by Sellafield over the years. Spent fuel does contain one material which the industry thinks has some uses – plutonium. Unfortunately, this is also notorious as one of the most toxic materials known to man.

Radiation poses two distinct threats to human health. In massive doses, as a result of nuclear explosions or major nuclear accidents, it can kill very quickly. It can destroy the body's central nervous system, make the stomach and intestines bleed badly and cause hair loss, nausea, prolonged vomiting and acute diarrhoea. It gives rise to bleeding under the skin, in the mouth and in the internal organs. It renders the body defenceless against infections. It effectively destroys the bone marrow – ironically the very feature that makes radiotherapy attractive as a method of treating leukaemia. The thirty-one fire-fighters, reactor physicists and technicians who died within weeks of the Chernobyl accident in Russia in 1986 suffered from some or all of these symptoms. So, obviously, did many thousands of those affected by the American bombing of the Japanese cities of Hiroshima and Nagasaki in 1945.

Much lower doses of radioactivity also harm health, although the precise effects are hard to quantify. It can injure life-giving cells, leading in the long term to cancers or genetic mutations. It can cause cataracts, skin damage and premature ageing. Although there is fierce controversy over the health impact of very low-level doses, it is now generally accepted that there is no threshold below which radiation can be said to be totally harmless. It follows that any increase in exposure to radiation, however slight, will increase an individual's chances of contracting cancer. But the disease may take years, even decades, to develop, thus often making it very difficult to prove that radiation is the cause. There is plenty of evidence from studies of people who survived the initial nuclear explosions in Hiroshima and Nagasaki to show how low levels of radiation can insidiously increase the risk of cancers, particularly leukaemia and bone marrow cancer. And the incidence of leukaemia amongst the first radiologists was nine times higher than normal. Marie Curie, who coined the term 'radioactivity', died at the age of sixty-seven from leukaemia caused by over-exposure to radiation, as did her daughter.

Sellafield, originally called Windscale, was rechristened by BNFL in 1981 in a vain attempt to improve its poor public image. A famous cartoon in the *Guardian* shortly after the Chernobyl nuclear accident showed one nuclear scientist from the former Soviet Union saying to another: 'We have sought advice from the United Kingdom and they suggest we change the name.' Sellafield's site, which is on the coast of the Lake District near Whitehaven in Cumbria, was first cleared in 1947 for the building of two military plutonium production reactors. They produced the plutonium that was used in Britain's first nuclear warheads, and their contaminated 400-foot chimneys still dominate the site.

Since then Sellafield has grown hugely, but it has always maintained a military as well as a civil function. It has separated and stockpiled plutonium for nuclear weapons in Britain and the USA as well as storing military waste, although many of the details are kept secret. Like a small town, it has about a hundred buildings, its own railway station and bus depot. It is the store for all Britain's high-level radioactive waste (1,400 cubic metres in twenty-one constantly cooled tanks in 1994) and all its separated civil plutonium (41 tonnes in 1994). Sellafield is being investigated as a possible site for an underground dump for medium-level waste. It is adjacent to the world's first electricity-producing nuclear power station at Calder Hall, which has also been used to produce plutonium for nuclear weapons.

What has gained Sellafield its notoriety is its main function: nuclear fuel reprocessing. This is the traditional way of dealing with the highly radioactive spent fuel from nuclear power stations. It is a chemical process which involves chopping up used fuel rods and dissolving them in acid. The purpose is to separate them into four main components: low-level waste, some of which is discharged into the environment and some of which is dumped at BNFL's licensed disposal site at Drigg a few miles from Sellafield; medium-level waste, which is stored at Sellafield awaiting the construction of an engineered underground dump; high-level waste, which remains toxic to life for hundreds of thousands of years and is scheduled to be stored on the site for at least the next fifty, awaiting a decision on its final disposal; and plutonium, which was meant to be the fuel for a new, more efficient generation of fast breeder reactors.

More than a thousand tonnes of spent fuel arrives at Sellafield for reprocessing every week from Britain's nuclear power stations, as well as from numerous other plants abroad. It is a truly international nuclear laundry, one of the world's only two large-scale nuclear reprocessing plants, the other being at Cap La Hague on the north coast of France. The only other reprocessing that has taken place in Britain has been at Dounreay fast reactor research establishment on the north coast of Scotland, and this has been on a small scale primarily for research purposes. At Sellafield there have been a series of major commercial reprocessing plants over the years, culminating with the Thermal Oxide Reprocessing Plant, otherwise known as THORP, which eventually opened in 1994 at a total cost of over £2.8 billion after two decades of intense controversy. THORP has been built to reprocess spent fuel from modern nuclear power stations in Britain, Germany, Japan and six other industrialised countries.

The nuclear industry puts forward two key arguments in favour of reprocessing: that it produces a valuable new fuel, plutonium; and that it eases the problem of nuclear waste disposal. I believe that both of these arguments are demonstrably wrong. Although plutonium has always been thought of by the industry as the nuclear fuel of the future, it now looks as if this will not turn out to be the case. Plutonium was meant to fuel a programme of new and different nuclear reactors known as fast breeders, which could theoretically increase the efficiency with which electricity is extracted from nuclear fuel. However, almost every attempt around the globe to develop a commercial fast breeder has run into insuperable economic and technical difficulties. The British effort centred at Dounreay has palpably failed, with the government committed to phasing out its considerable financial backing for the project during the 1990s. Apart from fuelling fast breeders, the only other major use for plutonium is in nuclear warheads. Personally, I do not think that the construction of weapons of mass destruction is politically or morally justifiable. Since the Cold War ended, it is difficult to see how they could have any practical use either.

Reprocessing does not ease the problems of nuclear waste disposal, it hugely augments them. According to independent analyses, the process actually increases the total volume of waste by a staggering 160 times. By separating it into several different categories it complicates rather than simplifies ultimate disposal. Reprocessing is in fact the dirtiest and most dangerous part of the whole business of nuclear power, threatening workers and public alike with risks from routine emissions and accidental leaks. It is also a totally unnecessary technology. The main alternative – storing unreprocessed spent fuel at the nuclear power stations where it is produced – is cheaper, safer and more convenient. That is why most other countries, including the USA and Germany, have abandoned the idea of reprocessing, and why Sellafield's main customers in Britain, the electricity boards, are trying to wriggle out of their future reprocessing commitments. When the House of Commons Environment Committee examined reprocessing in 1986, it concluded that most of the arguments in its favour had little merit. 'We are led to the conclusion,' said the committee, 'that the real reason why BNFL is anxious to go ahead with an expanded reprocessing programme is because it has done so in the past.'

The nuclear industry still has no real idea of what it is going to end up doing with the medium- and high-level radioactive wastes that result from reprocessing. Medium-level waste is meant to be dumped down a carefully designed deep hole which the Nuclear Industry Radioactive Waste Executive (Nirex) is currently researching near Sellafield. Several previous attempts to find a technically and politically acceptable disposal site have failed, and there are signs that Nirex's work at Sellafield is creating more problems than it is solving. The research timetable has already slipped by years because of unforeseen geological problems which could lead to the waste leaking into potential water supplies. High-level waste, which includes plutonium, is an even greater problem. Government policy is to leave this stored in tanks above ground for at least the next fifty years, despite some experts' suggestions that this could lead to an accident which would release large amounts of radioactivity. The eventual plan, such as it is, is to solidify the waste into glass blocks and then somehow dispose of them so that they will be isolated from the environment for hundreds of thousands of years. No one yet knows how and where this will be done.

But it is what has already happened to the so-called low-level waste that worries me most. As part of a deliberate policy, vast quantities of liquid waste have been pumped along Sellafield's two-mile pipeline into the open sea. For thirty years about a million gallons a day has poured through the pipeline, turning the Irish Sea and the Cumbrian coastline into one of the most radioactive environments in the world. The only areas that are worse are around the Chernobyl nuclear station in the Ukraine, and near other former Soviet nuclear sites. Scientific analysis has shown that every fish and every shellfish caught near Sellafield is contaminated with its radioactivity. Plutonium from the plant has been detected in sea spray, in the air, on beaches, up river estuaries, in house dust, in sheep and cattle – and even in tiny amounts in the bodies of local people. It has spread to the Solway Firth in Scotland, where it can be found at worrying levels in the river estuaries. In smaller concentrations, it has crept all around the Scottish coast and can even be measured in Sweden, Iceland and Greenland.

The official justification for such pollution has been the policy known as 'dilute and disperse', which assumed that the radioactivity would be harmlessly distributed out to the sea. But in fact the opposite seems to be happening. The plutonium and other pollutants are gradually being swept back to the shore by ocean currents, and deposited in dangerous amounts on the mudflats and river estuaries of Britain's north-west coast. The sea bed off Sellafield is reckoned to contain about three-quarters of a tonne of plutonium from discharges over the decades. This is going to carry on coming ashore and poisoning the environment for at least the next hundred thousand years. Other than dredging vast areas of the sea bed, evacuating coastal villages or banning fishing in the Irish Sea, there is little that can practically be done about it. An unparalleled and irretrievable environmental crime has been committed.

The extraordinary extent of the pollution was brought home to me in 1984 by a dramatic protest against Sellafield's discharges by Cumbrians Opposed to a Radioactive Environment. It took a dustbin full of mud from the Ravenglass estuary, five miles south of Sellafield, and dumped it in Whitehall, near the Prime Minister's official residence at 10 Downing Street. The area was immediately cordoned off by police, whose scientists were shocked at the levels of radioactivity they measured in the mud. It had to be carefully packaged up and disposed of as low-level radioactive waste at BNFL's licensed waste tip at Drigg, ironically near Ravenglass. The fact is that Ravenglass mud has been so contaminated with Sellafield's plutonium that, were it inside the plant, it would exceed the occupational safety limits and workers would be forbidden from touching it. Despite this, BNFL has always maintained that Sellafield's emissions pose no serious threat to the health of local people.

As well as all the planned pollution, accidents at the plant have led to disturbing and unexpected leaks of radioactivity. The worst accident took place in 1957 after one of the first nuclear reactors caught fire. This led to the release into the atmosphere of three-quarters of a million gigabecquerels of the radioactive gas iodine 131. The becquerel is now the standard unit for the measurement of radioactivity equivalent to the tiny amount of radiation emitted every second when a single atom decays. A gigabecquerel, on the other hand, is a billion becquerels: a very large amount of radioactivity. The release contaminated grass which was eaten by cows which in turn produced contaminated milk. As a result the government banned milk consumption from a 200 square-mile area around the plant. About two million litres of milk were collected and poured away to prevent anyone from drinking it. Although the authorities insisted at the time that no one would be harmed, the government's National Radiological Protection Board admitted in 1983 that the radioactive iodine released could 'in theory' cause 260 cases of thyroid cancer, thirteen of them fatal. In response to criticism that it had underestimated the number of potential deaths, the board subsequently increased its estimate of potential fatalities to thirty-three.

In 1973 there was an explosion in one of the reprocessing plants, creating a radioactive cloud which was blown back into the building and contaminated the lungs and skin of thirty-five workers. In 1976 excavation work accidentally uncovered a huge leak of radioactivity into the ground from a waste storage tank. About 1.8 million gigabecquerels of radioactivity was officially estimated to have leaked out over the previous four years, at a rate of 400 litres a day. In 1978 another spillage from a waste tank was discovered, amounting this time to more than 3.7 million gigabecquerels. In 1983, when I was pregnant with Gemma, there was the beach contamination incident which I described in Chapter 1.

After all these accidents official inquiries were set up which were very critical of BNFL's safety standards. The findings of a wide-ranging investigation by the government's Health and Safety Executive, published in 1981, were scathing:

> By the early 1970s the standard of the plants at Sellafield had deteriorated to an unsatisfactory level. We consider this represented a poor base line from which to develop high standards of safety. We are strongly of the opinion that such a situation should not have been allowed to develop, nor should it be permitted to occur again.

Another 'safety audit' by the same organisation five years later complained of the same problems. There were still, it concluded, 'deficiencies that could lead to hazards to the workers and in some limited circumstances to the public'. BNFL always promised to improve its performance, but the accidents continued. Between 1950 and 1986 there were a total of 274 potentially serious incidents at Sellafield.

The plant's radioactivity has been blamed for killing dozens of its own workers with cancer, often leukaemias like Gemma's. Malcolm Pattinson, a process worker there who had been regularly exposed to radiation over fourteen years, died of leukaemia at the age of thirty-six in 1971. Nine years later after a long legal battle his widow won £67,000 damages from BNFL, which for the first and only time admitted liability. The widow of Jonathon Troughton, who had died of bone marrow cancer in 1975 after being badly contaminated with plutonium, was awarded £22,441 by BNFL in a settlement agreed the day before the case was due in court. The widow of James Connor, who had died of myeloid leukaemia in 1976, was awarded £28,500 by the government. The widow of Geoffrey Southwood, who also died of myeloid leukaemia in 1975, was awarded £60,000 compensation by BNFL. Altogether up to 1981, BNFL had forked out nearly £200,000 for six former Sellafield workers. The company then agreed a compensation scheme for cancer victims with the trade unions, which has resulted in over £1 million being paid out to twenty-six families – without any admission of liability in any case and on condition that their names remained secret.

Taking a common-sense view, it seems to me that if a company is willing to give so much money to employees who believe that their work made them sick, it implies that it is accepting moral, if not legal, responsibility. It certainly undermines BNFL's line, which used to be frequently trotted out by faithful public relations staff, that no one had ever been killed by radiation from Britain's nuclear industry. During Gemma's illness I met the widow of a Sellafield worker who had died of leukaemia. I put her in touch with lawyers and she managed to win compensation within a year. I was glad for her, but I was left with a feeling of unfairness. If you became sick after working on the inside of the chicken wire fence that encircles Sellafield, BNFL would – at least sometimes – take responsibility for you. But if you were, say, a suffering young child who lived outside the fence, the company would ignore you. It was as if it believed that no wind, no rain and no radioactivity could ever penetrate its magic fence.

My husband Steven started work at Sellafield in 1977 as a 'chain boy' when he was seventeen, before I met him. Employed by contracting engineers Balfour Beatty, he initially helped with the construction of a new fuel-handling plant known as Pond 5. He was not issued with a radiation badge as the area was a green-field site classified by BNFL as clean, although it was only 200–300 yards from the Calder Hall reactors. When Steven turned eighteen, he was made a labourer and carried on working at the site until 1981, latterly employed by another contractor called Caxious.

After a short period on the dole, he next got a job in June 1981 with a firm of electrical contractors called Holliday Hall, for whom he worked until 1984. This involved working inside the chicken wire fence in controlled areas where radiation exposure was recognised as a potential risk. He first worked on the extension of a building known as B39, only discovering later that he was shielded from high radiation levels in the building by no more than a sheet of steel. Later he helped replace underground cables on the site by digging trenches between buildings.

On one job he was helping to dig a trench just outside the fence when a small dumper truck drove up on the inside towing a pneumatic drill. Less than thirty yards away from him three BNFL men got out and put on transparent plastic suits and face masks which were meant to provide protection from radiation. Someone else arrived with a geiger counter and started to monitor a path. He indicated an area to the others who then proceeded to hammer out about two cubic feet of tarmac and dirt, creating a large dust cloud in the process. All the rubble was carefully put in plastic bags, which, like all solid low-level radioactive waste, were disposed of at the Drigg waste tip. One of Steven's workmates asked the man with the geiger counter what had happened. He said that radioactive contamination had mysteriously appeared on the path, which led to changing rooms used by BNFL workers.

On another occasion he had to fit electronic surveillance security cameras on the roof of a plutonium store. This involved going inside the store, which was only permitted with a police escort. Once, when Steven and some other workers were waiting for the escort to arrive, he got a real fright. A man in a white coat pushed a small two-wheeled trolley no bigger than a football past the radiation detector, and set off every alarm in the building. 'That really scared me, and after that I avoided going in there unless I had to,' he told me.

After he was made redundant by Holiday Hall in 1984, he was unemployed for twelve months. In 1985 he was taken on by Bexter Engineering to help with the construction of a waste treatment facility known as SIXEP, which had concrete walls four feet thick. This was meant to be in a safe area, but once when he was talking to a BNFL supervisor the man's radiation alarm started bleeping. 'When he looked at the reading, he turned visibly white and told us to get the hell out of the building as there had been a site emergency,' Steven recalled.

> We ran out to our cabin, shut the windows and doors, got out our emergency face masks and waited for the site alarm to sound. After about fifteen minutes nothing had happened and one of our foremen came and asked what was going on. When we told him, he said he would find out what was happening. He came back after five minutes and suggested that someone had been having us on. We refused to move from the cabin and stayed there for one and a half hours. Then two BNFL men and our big boss came and told us that there had been a leak in a building, but it had been contained and no site emergency had been declared. We then went back to work, but were told later that some radioactivity had leaked out and been blown across the site and out to sea.

After that incident workers began to mistrust BNFL, which only issued radiation badges to those who worked in controlled areas where radiation exposure was considered a risk. Some of Steven's colleagues who worked outside such areas brought in their own badges – radiation-sensitive sections of photographic film encased in plastic, which are commonly available. They then compared the radiation doses on their badges with the doses recorded on the badges issued by BNFL. The doses Steven's colleagues were receiving seemed similar to those received by workers in the designated radioactive zones. 'We found out later that the Calder Hall reactors, which were opposite our cabins, were emitting radiation – so even men who were working in clean areas were getting quite high doses,' Steven said.

When the SIXEP contract was completed in 1987, Steven was moved back to radioactively controlled areas, which by then he hated. The practice was to work two hours inside and two hours outside these areas, although if workers reached their permitted dose levels for the day they would be kept out. He was involved in replacing stainless steel pipes inside radioactive reprocessing cells that were shut down for the duration. The work had to be done wearing protective plastic suits and face masks. When the pipes were being cut with grinders, by the light of halogen lamps he could see tiny particles of the radioactive metal floating in the air. He used to worry about whether the filter in his mask was really fine enough to prevent him from breathing them in.

He recounted one occasion on which a general foreman, who was regularly ribbed by his employees for being afraid of radiation, had to enter a controlled area. He put on some protective overshoes, a white laboratory coat and walked around organising the day's tasks without his hands ever leaving his pockets. On his way out, he took off his shoes, washed his hands and put them in the radiation monitor. After a few seconds the alarm went off, suggesting that he was contaminated. He refused to believe it, but was advised by the changing room attendant to call in the health inspectors. They arrived after about ten minutes and checked him over with a geiger counter. It started off just ticking like a loud clock, but ended up buzzing continually like an angry bee. Visibly distressed, the man had to be scrubbed until he was deemed decontaminated.

The more I found out about the pollution, the accidents and the risks faced by workers, the more I began to wonder whether Sellafield might be to blame for Gemma's illness. Despite the horror stories he told, Steven was more sceptical, refusing to believe that his work could have harmed her. Increasingly we started to argue about it. He maintained that there were other possible causes of leukaemia such as smoking, chemicals, viruses or inherited conditions. I pointed out that radiation was a known cause of leukaemia and that we lived and he worked in one of the world's most radioactively contaminated areas. I found it difficult to believe this was just a coincidence. My suspicions were reinforced as I learned more about the large number of people in the area who seemed to suffer from cancer.

When I lived in London I never heard of a single case of leukaemia, even when I was in school with two thousand other children. But as soon as I moved to Cumbria, it seemed as if three-quarters of the people whom I heard had died were cancer victims. The first case of leukaemia I heard about in Cleator Moor was a little boy who went to the school to which Gemma would have gone. The second was a little girl whose mother my sister met when she was selling her house. I was so sad when I heard that they had both died. I heard of other cases three miles away, in Egremont. Then there was all the publicity about the 'cluster' of cases in Seascale, the small coastal village immediately adjacent to Sellafield. I even got annoyed at all the media focus on Seascale, as if the cancers were somehow confined to the one place. After Gemma was diagnosed, I met more and more local people who had the same type of leukaemia as her, other leukaemias or other cancers. I am still meeting them.

Although there had long been gossip about alleged excesses of cancer in Cumbria, there was never any hard evidence. Every time an official body like the local health authority analysed the figures, it came to the conclusion that West Cumbria's cancer rates were the same as or lower than the national average. It was not until November 1983, with the broadcast of Yorkshire Television's documentary *Windscale: the Nuclear Laundry*, that things changed – and changed dramatically. The programme, produced by James Cutler whom I later got to know well, revealed that five children under ten had contracted leukaemia in Seascale between 1954 and 1983 – ten times the national average. The cancer rate amongst children under fifteen for the whole coastal area to the south of Sellafield was five times the national average.

The programme caused a national outcry, prompting the then prime minister, Margaret Thatcher, to launch an immediate inquiry under a respected public health expert, Sir Douglas Black. The response of BNFL was predictably hostile, although I was surprised at the role played by one of the consultants who had diagnosed Gemma, Dr Alan Craft. He publicly insisted that his statistics showed no increase in the incidence of childhood cancer in Cumbria. But he seemed to me to make the same mistake as the health authority officials who had offered the original reassurances. The whole point of James Cutler's programme was that the high rates of cancer were only detectable if small enough areas were analysed. Large area analyses, such as for the whole of Cumbria, averaged out – and therefore overlooked – local excesses.

When Sir Douglas Black's report was published in 1984, its tone was overwhelmingly reassuring. It concluded that it was impossible to prove or disprove the theory that Sellafield was responsible for the high rates of childhood leukaemia in the local area. But it added: 'We have found no evidence of any general risk to health for children or adults living near Sellafield when compared to the rest of Cumbria, and we can give a qualified reassurance to the people who are concerned about a possible health hazard in the neighbourhood of Sellafield.' The nuclear industry breathed a collective sigh of relief, feeling that it had been let off the hook. Its sweet-tongued public relations operatives took to presenting the report's 'qualified reassurance' as a clean bill of health for Sellafield. Sometimes, the nuclear frontmen let their real feelings show. The remarks made in January 1985 by Sir John Hill, the president of the industry lobby group, British Nuclear Forum, I found personally offensive. 'Let us hope,' he said, 'that the Black Report stops once and for all the parading of weeping relatives of cancer victims in front of the television cameras saying: "It must be due to Sellafield."'

Part of the Black Report's argument was based on a study carried out by the government's National Radiological Protection Board (NRPB). It worked out how many leukaemia deaths the known emissions of radioactivity from Sellafield would be expected to cause, using the conventional risk assumptions ultimately derived from observations of the effects of the atomic bombs dropped on Japan in 1945. Since the number of real deaths was much higher than the number expected, the NRPB concluded – and the Black Report accepted – that radiation could not be to blame. This seems to me to be a totally crazy argument. Carried to its logical extreme, it would imply that the more people from around Sellafield who died from leukaemia, the less likely radiation from the plant would be to blame. I think it would have been much more sensible to have questioned the accuracy of the conventional risk assessments and to have started looking for hitherto unknown ways in which low levels of radiation can harm people.

It would also have been a good idea to have been rather more sceptical about the official figures on Sellafield's discharges over the years. One of the outcomes of the Black Report was the establishment of a new government advisory body called the Committee on Medical Aspects of Radiation in the Environment, better known as COMARE. Its first report, published in 1986, concluded that there had been a huge release of radioactivity from Sellafield which had not been disclosed to the authors of the Black Report. Corroding fuel cans and ineffectual filters caused about 20 kilograms of uranium oxide to leak into the atmosphere in the mid-1950s. The leak was only revealed because a lone nuclear industry scientist, Dr Derek Jakeman, drew attention to it. COMARE's conclusion wrecked the nuclear establishment's credibility:

> The way in which these data came to light is unsatisfactory and undermines our confidence in the adequacy and completeness of the available data . . . we feel that the monitoring programme and record-keeping for the 1950s were such that we cannot be certain that all releases have now been recognised. We therefore consider that the level of uncertainty about the information available and about the risk to the population from the Sellafield

discharges is now greater than at the time of the publication of the Black Report.

Further disturbing evidence came with the publication in 1987 of a Scottish Office study of the incidence of childhood leukaemia around Britain's only other nuclear reprocessing plant, at Dounreay in northern Scotland. The study found five people under the age of twenty-five who had suffered leukaemia between 1979 and 1984 and who had lived within 12.5 kilometres of Dounreay. This, Scottish Office health researchers pointed out, was ten times greater than the national average and extremely unlikely to have been caused by chance. They drew attention to the striking similarities between the cluster of cases at Dounreay and the cluster already identified around Sellafield, as well as a third suspected cluster close to the Aldermaston nuclear weapons facility in Berkshire. Taken together, they concluded, 'there does appear to be a cause for concern'.

Another study, carried out as a result of the Black Report by Professor Martin Gardner from Southampton University and Dr John Terrell, West Cumbria's district medical officer, concluded in 1987 that 'the excess of leukaemia among Seascale children is confirmed'. They said that children born in Seascale were ten times more likely to die of leukaemia than average, and three times more likely to die of other cancers. They also revealed that three Seascale cases – one leukaemia and two other cancers – had been left out of the original analysis carried out for the Black Report. This was because the people concerned had left Seascale before their conditions were diagnosed.

In the light of the new evidence that emerged in the wake of his report, Sir Douglas Black changed his mind. He said in 1987 that there was a 'high likelihood' that in small areas near Sellafield there was an increased risk of leukaemia in young children. He described the evidence of high leukaemia rates around other nuclear installations as 'disquieting'. There was now, he said, 'quite a likelihood that there is a genuine link' between nuclear plants and childhood leukaemias. Researchers around the world, particularly in Germany and North America, began investigating possible links between nuclear plants and local excesses of childhood leukaemia.

British Nuclear Fuels continued to deny everything. I saw their spokespeople dozens of times on the television, and they were always trying to play the whole issue down. Every time there was another leak they would make the same bland, reassuring noises. I found myself getting increasingly frustrated by the company's attitude. When I talked to local people, many of them privately agreed that the plant was probably to blame. But hardly anyone was prepared to say so publicly. Like me, they were caught in an impossible Catch 22. They were worried about the leaks of radioactivity and their impact upon the health of the community, but at the same time they were conscious of everyone's economic dependence on Sellafield. They knew that their jobs and their income were gained from an occupation that could be killing children, but they put their jobs first and chose to keep quiet about it. It was becoming plain to me, however, that I was going to have to make a different choice.

When I talked to a woman who was active in a local anti-nuclear group, I learnt something very interesting. In 1958 John Dunster, the scientist initially in charge of health and safety at Sellafield, had submitted a remarkably honest paper to a United Nations conference in Geneva on the peaceful uses of atomic energy. His attitude to the huge amounts of radioactive pollution that the plant had pumped down its pipeline into the Irish Sea during the first six years of its life was alarming, to say the least:

> The sea has always been regarded by coastal and seafaring people as the ideal place for dumping their waste and this is, of course, a very reasonable and proper attitude . . . Most of the objects which ultimately do find their way to the shore are harmless and a considerable source of pleasure to children.
>
> Not the least of the attractions of the sea as a dumping ground has been the lack of administrative controls . . . The intention has been to discharge fairly substantial amounts of radioactivity as part of an organised and deliberate scientific experiment . . . the aims of this experiment would have been

> defeated if the level of radioactivity discharged had been kept to a minimum.

The truth was beginning to dawn on me. Sellafield had knowingly dumped excessive amounts of radioactivity in my environment. It was me and everyone else who lived in West Cumbria who were the guinea pigs in the nuclear industry's 'deliberate scientific experiment'. More particularly, it was our children. It was my Gemma's life that was being sacrificed.

Chapter 5

Dying but Not Ill

'It fits, Grandad, it fits! Look.' Gemma was twirling round excitedly in the middle of the room, showing off the beautiful white and red christening dress which my father had just given her. Only the prospect of putting on the matching new ankle socks persuaded her to sit down. 'What's that like?' she demanded, bouncing up again to flaunt herself like a model on a catwalk.

'I don't know. There's still something missing,' said Dad, as if he could not quite put his finger on it. 'Ah, I know.'

'What?' asked Gemma, genuinely puzzled. From out of a box Dad pulled a pair of shining blood-red patent leather shoes. 'Mum, look! Shocking shoes! Red ones!' Beside herself with joy, she flung her arms around Grandad's neck and thanked him.

Ever since we had told her that she was going to be christened along with her cousin Bianca, Gemma had been very excited. As well as a new outfit, it meant a party, lots of food and – most important of all – being the centre of attention. It was my father's idea, born of his Italian Catholic conviction. He was bothered that, unless she was christened, she could not have a proper Catholic burial. He pointed out, too, that I and my sisters had all been christened as Catholics, even though our mother was not a Catholic. Neither Steven nor I were particularly religious. We had not had Gemma christened because we had reckoned that she would have to decide for herself, when she was older, what religion, if any, she wanted to follow. But, now that her future seemed foreshortened, it had somehow become more important.

At very short notice we booked a priest, and a nearby hotel for a meal. Steven's younger brother, Ian, agreed to be Gemma's godfather and Tina her godmother, while Steven and I played the same roles for Bianca. My mother was coming up from London and I was anxious because she and my father had not parted on good terms. My father promised to call a truce for the day, which he did by buying her a bottle of wine. There was also some tension with Steven's parents over the arrangements, but everything was sorted out all right in the end.

On the big day Gemma and Bianca acted as if they were getting married. Richenda was lovely too in a blue, yellow and pink pinstriped pinafore and white tee-shirt which I had bought her. She actually looked like a little girl instead of the tomboy image she had been cultivating. Because there were two children being christened at the same time, the ceremony itself was a little confusing. When the priest asked the respective parents and godparents to touch the children's heads, all our hands became tangled up. At the end the priest gave Gemma, who was an official member of the Worzel Gummidge Fan Club, a present which she loved: a hand-knitted Worzel with a tiny mouse sown on to his shoulder. 'Look after that little mouse, Gemma,' said the priest, 'and you'll always have good luck.'

That evening, for once, Gemma went upstairs to bed without argument. 'Night, Mam. Love ya.'

'Love you too, Gem,' I responded.

'Sleep tight and watch the bed bugs don't bite,' she continued.

'Sleep, Gem. Dream about your christening.' I was walking down the stairs.

'Love ya. Love you too, Dad,' she shouted. For two or three minutes she kept shouting, then we knew by the silence that she had fallen asleep. She slept like a baby. It had been a good day, despite the fact that every time I looked at her the word 'leukaemia' leaped into my mind. We had to learn to make every day as special.

Since coming home after those traumatic four days of diagnosis at Newcastle Infirmary, I had been trying to accustom myself to the idea that my healthy-looking child was very sick, trying to understand exactly what was happening inside her. Tina told me she had been to the library and looked up 'chronic myeloid leukaemia' in a couple of medical dictionaries. On average the disease affected about 650 people every year in the United Kingdom, only about fifteen of whom were children. The three other main types of leukaemia – acute myeloid, acute lymphoblastic and chronic lymphocytic – had survival rates of between 40 and 80 per cent, whereas a mere 10 per cent of those with chronic myeloid leukaemia could hope to live – and then only with the aid of a successful bone marrow transplant.

Leukaemia, or blood cancer, is basically the breakdown of the bone marrow. The bone marrow's job is to manufacture blood cells in sufficient quantity and in the right balance to enable the rest of the body to function properly. This it normally does with extraordinary efficiency, producing about three million red blood cells and 120,000 white blood cells every second. The red cells, which give blood its colour, contain a protein called haemoglobin which carries oxygen to all the tissues in the body. The white cells, which include a variety of different types including neutrophils, play a vital role in combating infection. The bone marrow also produces another type of cell called platelets, which enable blood to clot and thus stem bleeding. The balance of different types of cells within the blood, which is essential for good health, is measured by a 'blood count' derived from analysing small samples of blood. When infected by leukaemia the bone marrow starts producing large numbers of abnormal blood cells, usually white ones. These leukaemic cells take over the bone marrow, spill out into the bloodstream and spread throughout the body, wreaking havoc wherever they go. The whole balance of the blood, and hence the body, is disturbed and ultimately destroyed.

Chronic myeloid leukaemia is a slow-progressing form of the disease which particularly affects one of the main types of white blood cell, known as granulocytes. It is characterised by an unusually high number of granulocytes at all stages of development circulating in the blood. Its chronic phase, which can last several years, is invariably followed by an acute phase, which can rapidly become fatal. Scientists have discovered that every bone marrow cell infected with chronic myeloid leukaemia contains an abnormal chromosome, known as the 'Philadelphia chromosome' after the city where it was first described in 1960. This chromosome, which carries the genetic information of the cell, has one mutant gene, obscurely termed the BCR/ABL gene. No one is sure what causes this gene to mutate.

Other people were lucky that they did not have to understand such arcane matters. But sometimes their thoughtlessness made it harder for me to come to terms with Gemma's condition. The first day we were back from Newcastle, we were on the way to the local doctor when we saw walking down the other side of the road a woman whom I had known vaguely for years. News – especially bad news – travels fast in a small community like Cleator Moor. She stopped and shouted that she thought Gemma was in hospital in Newcastle. She was, I called back, but we came home yesterday. 'Oh, that's good. I'm glad she's better now,' said the woman and walked off. I was so shocked that I did not have the heart to correct her.

Often I felt as if people were staring at us, gossiping about us, almost gloating over our fate, although that was probably mostly my imagination. It was hard to accept that other people's lives were still the same, that they still carried on doing the things they had always been doing. For a while I think I wandered around in a kind of strange daze, feeling as if everyone else was moving in slow motion. The extraordinary thing was that Gemma carried on living her little life to the limit much as she had always done. She played endlessly outdoors with Bianca and Helen's identical twins from next door. She always seemed lively, energetic, hungry and happy. Every time I told people that Gemma had leukaemia, they remarked on how well she was looking, as if I was making a mountain out of a molehill. The contrast between my understanding of what was wrong with her inside and the outward appearance that everything was all right became very depressing after a while. We just had to keep giving her the pills and keep an eye on her. It was as if she was dying but not ill.

The need to isolate her from infections caused several problems, some minor, some major. We tried not to wrap her in cotton wool, but it was not easy. Shopping one quiet day in the local supermarket with Gemma sitting in the trolley, we could not avoid a little boy who was coughing and sneezing the whole time. Wherever we went he and his father always seemed to be close by. Eventually Steven insisted that we could not take any more chances and had to leave. We parked the trolley, part-full of unpaid-for shopping, and went home. It was not the boy's fault; he could have just had a mild infection. But a mild infection to a healthy young boy could have been a killer virus to Gemma. After that we tried to keep her away from crowds as much as possible.

Steven and I both had to decide how much to carry on working, him at Sellafield and me at the packaging factory, Mardons Composites. He soon went back to work, and his employer at the time, Bexter Engineering, was very sympathetic to the days he needed off for hospital visits. I kept postponing any decision as to what I should do, and my employer was very understanding too. About three months after Gemma was diagnosed I did try and go back to work at the factory, but handed in my notice after just half an hour. I could not handle it. It seemed so much more important to spend time with Gemma, given that her time with us could be so short.

In between the strange days at home, we had to visit the hospital in Newcastle every few weeks. It developed into a kind of ritual. Steven would take the day off work and we would usually leave early. About half an hour out of Newcastle we always passed a gigantic strawberry in a field, which was how Gemma knew we were nearly there. We always said we would stop one day to pick our own strawberries, but we never seemed to find the time. At the hospital they would expertly take a blood sample from Gemma and give her a drumstick lolly. The consultant now overseeing treatment – a middle-aged woman with silver-grey hair called Dr Jenny Kernahan, who had an impressive and professional manner – would then check her over, feeling her stomach and looking into her eyes. Normally she would tell us that Gemma's blood count was holding up well and that the treatment with busulphan seemed to be working and should be continued.

On the way back we would pull over at a Little Chef for something to eat. Gemma would always ask for a dish called Cosmic Chicken, which consisted of chicken breast in breadcrumbs, chips and peas, but she would hardly ever finish it. Then she would fall asleep in the car until we got home. In the evening we seemed to spend most of the time on the phone, telling relatives and friends what had happened. More often than not, it was very little. But every detail was pored over, examined and re-examined, discussed and rediscussed, to see what few grains of hope might be extracted from it. I sometimes became frustrated that I never had any really good news to tell anyone. I would have loved to have come home and been able to say that the doctors had checked Gemma over and suddenly realised that their diagnosis had all been a huge mistake.

One visit to Newcastle was particularly memorable because Steven, Richenda and I all agreed to have blood samples taken to see if any of us could be suitable bone marrow donors. We had to get up very early, and the children bickered all the way in the back of the car. They were both boasting about how brave they would be. At the hospital I volunteered to give blood first, thinking that I could show the children how little it was going to hurt. Dr Kernahan prepared a tray with sterile bottles, cotton wool and swabs, and then tied a long rubber belt around the top of my arm. She asked me to make a fist and studied my veins. Telling me to look away, she used a butterfly needle to pierce my skin and then with a 50 millilitre syringe drew out enough blood to fill two or three pots. Under the constant gaze of Gemma and Richenda, I tried to look calm, but it was difficult. They kept asking whether it hurt. 'No, not at all,' I said, trying to sound convincing.

It was Richenda's turn next and she looked petrified. Gemma stared solemnly at her, with one eye on the butterfly needle and the other on Richenda's face, watching for the first tear. Richenda tried desperately to hold back the tears when she felt the prick, but she failed. It was cruel to watch. When it came to Gemma's turn, she had to sit on my knee. She kept pulling her arm away when the needle was about to be inserted, until Richenda, now recovered, teased her for being a baby. When it was over, she quickly wiped away her tears.

Throughout all this Steven, who hates needles, had been sitting in the next room so he did not have to watch. Rather reluctantly he came through to the treatment room when I called him. 'Come on, Dad,' said Gemma, grinning. 'It doesn't hurt.' But as soon as Dr Kernahan started drawing blood, the colour drained from Steven's face. He was trying to look unconcerned in front of the children, but I could tell he was feeling faint. Dr Kernahan noticed too. Immediately she had finished, she fetched him a pillow and made him bend over and lay his head down until he felt better. Gemma started to look very worried. I tried to reassure her that he was just tired after the long drive. I was glad Steven had gone last.

We left the hospital feeling relieved that the ordeal was over and excited by the thought that we might have done something to help Gemma. We had been told that we would be very lucky to find a match amongst us as only one in four siblings – excepting identical twins – was on average suitable. We knew that we had to take it one step at a time and that the results would take two or three weeks to come through. But even if none of our bone marrow was like Gemma's, we had many friends and relatives who had also offered to be tested. Driving home, we could not help feeling distinctly happy. Hope was a tremendous tonic.

In the back of the car, Gemma and Richenda started demanding lunch at the Little Chef. Steven played dumb, so the two girls started sticking their tongues out at him behind his back and giggling. When we came over the brow of the hill and saw the café, the kids sat bolt upright, shouting: 'There it is, Dad, there it is.' Steven smirked at me and I guessed what he was going to do. He drove straight past the entrance, at which the girls both burst into tears. After prolonging the torture for a few more seconds with assumed innocence, Steven capitulated and turned back to the Little Chef.

'That was not funny, Dad.' Gemma gave her verdict before tucking into her Cosmic Chicken. 'It's nice here, isn't it, Mam?'

Unfortunately the tonic of hope was very short-lived. The next time we made the trek to Newcastle, Dr Kernahan told us that the analysis of our blood samples revealed that none of our bone marrows was exactly the same as Gemma's. Without a perfect match of cell tissue, her body would be bound to reject any transplanted material as 'foreign', with potentially fatal consequences. The transplanted tissue itself can also reject the host tissue, causing a very dangerous condition called 'graft versus host disease'. There was still a chance that a match could be found from someone on the register of willing donors, but that was very unlikely. I sat there and wiped my face, trying to hold back the tears. All the way home I dared not talk to Steven about my thoughts, because I knew Gemma would be listening in the back of the car. I did not want to scare her. While she was looking fit and feeling fine, I tried just to take whatever was thrown at me. It was only after we had put her and Richenda to bed that evening that I unburdened myself.

'She's going to die, isn't she?' I said, looking at Steven.

He tried to comfort me by pointing out that we would fight every inch of the way for Gemma. There was no way we could just sit back and accept what was happening to her. We had to do everything we could to try and save her life. I knew he was right. I had felt for some time that we ought to seek a second medical opinion on her condition. Steven had initially argued that Gemma was already in the best hands, but I still needed convincing. I suppose I also wanted another straw to clutch on to. When I made the request to Dr Kernahan she did not seem pleased, but agreed to write to a colleague, Dr Chessells, at Great Ormond Street Hospital in London. For weeks nothing happened, despite my continual asking, and I got increasingly anxious and impatient.

It was my health visitor, Joyce – one of the few who devoted time to my psychological health instead of Gemma's physical illness – who suggested that I should ring Great Ormond Street myself. After one of her weekly visits, I picked up the phone and asked Directory Enquiries for the hospital's number. I wrote it down, made a cup of tea and thought about what I should say. Then, with my heart beating fast, I dialled the number. I was rapidly put through to Dr Chessells' secretary, and after a short delay to the woman herself. She was about to go into a meeting, so our conversation was brief and businesslike. But to my great surprise and relief she agreed to see Gemma within a week, on Wednesday,

2 December 1987. When I put the phone down I was feeling very pleased with myself.

I broke the news to Steven that evening, grinning all over my face. He urged me not to build up my hopes too much, warning me that the second opinion could be exactly the same as the first. But I could not help feeling excited. I was making plans to stay with my mother in London, to take the children to the zoo and show them the sights. For the first time since Gemma was diagnosed, it felt as if I had something to celebrate, some genuinely good news to impart. I phoned everyone and told them. I am not sure what I was really expecting to learn from a second opinion. But there was undoubtedly a part of me that was yearning for the impossible: 'We're happy to tell you, Mrs D'Arcy, that it has all been a big mistake. Gemma does not have leukaemia after all . . .' I even pictured myself phoning friends to tell them, organising the celebratory party and starting to live our lives again.

Three days before we were due at Great Ormond Street, I had finished bathing Gemma and was fastening her dress when I noticed clusters of little spots on her back. Gemma pointed out some on her legs, too. They looked strange, as if they were under the surface of the skin, and seemed to be spreading. I was very worried because I thought it might be measles, which could be very dangerous. I rang the local hospital and was told to bring Gemma in immediately for a check-up. After an examination and a few questions, a doctor told me it was definitely not measles, but a condition known as petechiae – small burst blood vessels under the skin. It had probably been caused by rubbing her too hard with the towel after her bath, he said.

Because Steven had missed so much work recently, we couldn't afford the £90 train fares to London and had to borrow the money from my father. Gemma and Richenda, both laden with pocket money from Tina and their grandparents, were very excited as it was their first trip on a train. We enjoyed ourselves immensely during the four-hour journey – drawing, talking, eating and joking. At one point Gemma upset her elder sister by cheekily revealing their respective nicknames. 'My friends call me Gemma the Pemma,' she said, shrinking away from Richenda's threatening grasp. 'She is called Pain in D'Arcy.' For the first time in ages we felt like a real family.

The children were wide-eyed when we arrived in London. Everything seemed so big and crowded, and there were shops everywhere and stairs that moved. We took a black cab to my mother's home, where she ran a small but comfortable bed-and-breakfast business. When she opened the door, Gemma flung her arms around her, shouting, 'Hello, Nanna London!' and asked after her dog, Trixi. My mother was very pleased to see us, but as full of mixed feelings as Steven and myself. She promised to come to Great Ormond Street with us. 'You never know, you might get better news tomorrow,' she told me.

Up early the following morning, I put Gemma into a plain pink dress and talked enthusiastically about what we would do after we had been to the hospital. I combed her hair up into a pony-tail. When I had finished, she hugged me and told me she loved me. 'I love you too, Gem,' I replied.

When we arrived at the hospital, Gemma and Richenda thought it was a thrilling place. Pictures of Bambi and Snow White adorned the doors, other cartoon characters covered the walls and there were lavish play areas. While we waited in the reception area, the children played in a large Wendy house with a toy phone box large enough for them to stand up in.

Gemma had to give another blood sample, which she did after the usual struggle. We had to wait for what seemed like an eternity before her name was called out to see Dr Chessells. As we walked in, my stomach started to churn with excitement. After asking us to describe everything that had happened so far, she started examining Gemma. I asked her about chronic myeloid leukaemia and she confirmed that its survival rate was about 10 per cent, much lower than for other leukaemias. She described it as 'very rare' in anyone under forty years of age.

'What causes it?' I asked.

'No one really knows,' she said, peering closely at Gemma's skin.

'Could it be because we live near Sellafield and Steven works there?' This provoked a reproachful look from Steven.

Dr Chessells, whose mind was clearly on something else, never answered. She asked me instead about the small spots under Gemma's skin. I reported what I had been told by my local hospital, and she frowned. She asked a nurse to take Gemma with her to fetch the results of the blood test, and then dropped her bombshell. She said she was worried that the petechiae under the skin could mean that Gemma's condition had suddenly and dramatically deteriorated. Unless urgent remedial action was taken, she would be lucky to survive three weeks, never mind three years.

I felt panic and fear rising within me. This was not what I had come all this way to hear. All the small joys and tiny hopes that I had felt since getting an appointment at Great Ormond Street were crushed in an instant. Dr Chessells explained that the petechiae, which were small haemorrhages under the skin, meant that Gemma's blood was running out of platelets, the blood-clotting agents. This suggested that her bone marrow was beginning to malfunction seriously, probably as a direct result of the busulphan she was taking, leaving her without an effective immune system. The results of the blood test confirmed Dr Chessells' suspicions, and she telephoned Dr Kernahan to discuss what to do. Dr Chessells then recommended that we take Gemma immediately back to the Royal Victoria Infirmary in Newcastle to have her bone marrow tested. She stressed the importance of keeping Gemma away from crowds.

Feeling emotional, I thanked her and pointed out that, if we had not come, we would not have discovered what was happening. 'I was told I was an over-anxious mother,' I said.

'And don't be anything else, Mrs D'Arcy,' she replied smiling. Steven took hold of Gemma's hand as she skipped off down the corridor to find Nanna London and Richenda. When my mother asked how it had gone, my eyes filled and I just shook my head. She gave the children some money to go and buy snacks and I poured out the story. I felt angry and betrayed by the local hospital. If I had not arranged for a second opinion, it could have been two or three weeks before we had discovered the significance of the spots at our next scheduled appointment in Newcastle. Gemma could have died in that time. From then on I determined not to let medical staff get away with anything. If I did not understand anything, I would make them repeat it until I did. If I was concerned about anything, I would make sure I had the opinion of at least two doctors.

We had to abandon the proposed day out at London Zoo, a decision that produced ten minutes of tears from Gemma and Richenda. But they were soon rejuvenated by the prospect of another long train journey home. As we were saying goodbye to my mother, her lip began to tremble. I begged her not to break down in front of the children. I tried to sound optimistic. 'Come up and see us soon. Or if you can't, we'll be back when Gemma's better,' I said, although both of us knew that might never happen.

All the way home, and then on the way over to Newcastle, we tried to keep Gemma away from crowds. We also had to deprive her of food in preparation for the bone marrow test. As a result she was not in the best of moods when Dr Kernahan eventually came to see her in her hospital bed. She glowered fiercely at her. 'I was going to the zoo but we had to come here. I hate it here. And I'm hungry,' she complained.

When the porter came for Gemma with a surgical trolley, she refused to lie down. She sat up all the way along the corridors, watching people watching her. She screamed in protest at having to drink what the anaesthetist called 'magic milk', but then went straight to sleep. Steven and I walked over to the hospital café to have a cup of coffee while we were waiting. Then I looked at books in the hospital library, particularly the ones that tried to explain cancer in words of one syllable to children. How glad I was that my father had insisted on having Gemma christened. I asked Steven what we would do if we were told that she only had three weeks to live.

'Live life to the full,' he replied, 'but we'll cross that bridge when we come to it.'

It seemed ages before Gemma came back from the theatre, and when she did she was being carried in the arms of the anaesthetist, still in his green pants and overshirt, with his white face mask hanging around his neck. 'My arms feel like they're going to drop off,' he panted as he laid Gemma on the bed. He said he had carried her because it was quicker and safer than using the hospital lift. He asked us to try and keep Gemma mobile when she woke up. 'She's all right, but she'll be stiff. We had to go in quite deep.'

After an hour we had to wake Gemma up. A nurse leaned over her and started to call her name. Gemma turned away as if trying to shut out the voice. The nurse, still calling her name, gently shook her. Gemma grunted and groaned. 'Get off me, I'm tired!' she shouted, pulling back her leg ready to kick. We reassured the nurse that such aggression was entirely normal. I said that if Gemma was polite I would start to worry. When we eventually managed to get her to sit up, she complained that her leg was sore. Then she was sick all over her bedclothes and the floor. After we had cleaned up, she drank a few sips of water and fell asleep again.

Later on, when she woke again, she demolished two bowls of cereal and some toast. She said she was feeling tired and sore and wanted to go home. We carried her into the corridor and stood her gently on her feet to practise walking. She started to cry, demanding that Steven carry her again. But although it hurt, she managed to walk back to the ward where Dr Kernahan was waiting. The test had confirmed Dr Chessells' suspicion: Gemma's bone marrow had collapsed. But Dr Kernahan's news was not all bleak: there were still some healthy cells left which could aid recovery. She thought, as Dr Chessells had, that the collapse had actually been caused by the busulphan tablets that Gemma had been taking, so she recommended stopping the tablets for a while to see if the bone marrow recovered. She warned us again to keep Gemma away from any possible sources of infection, and said we could go home straightaway if we wanted to.

Gemma was delighted that we were going home, but I felt terrified inside. What if her bone marrow failed to recover? Dr Kernahan had given us no guarantees that it definitely would. During the drive home Gemma, as usual, demanded a stop at the Little Chef, but we were so worried about her catching infections that we refused. We stopped at a burger van in a lay-by instead, and kept Gemma in the car. For the next two weeks, we took particular care to try to isolate her from infections. This meant that we kept having to stop her playing with her friends whenever they had a cough or cold. She almost got used to us saying no all the time.

When we went back to Newcastle the next time, Dr Kernahan smiled when she received the results of the blood test. In the absence of busulphan Gemma's bone marrow was beginning to recover. Steven and I were hugely relieved. Now we seemed to be back where we were, talking about years of life instead of weeks. We discussed the chances of finding a suitable bone marrow donor, which seemed to be receding. I suggested advertising on the television, but Dr Kernahan said it was not like other transplants. There had to be a precise match, and that was very hard to find. I told her that we had considered having another baby, if that would help. But we knew that it would be unfair on the baby if he or she were conceived just to be a donor for an elder sister. We would really have to want another child. Dr Kernahan agreed, and pointed out that in any case it was far from certain that a new sibling would provide a perfect match.

As well as my struggle for a second opinion, I had two other unexpected struggles on my hands: one for a nursery place and the other for an attendance allowance. My attempt to get Gemma into nursery was not helped initially by a stupid mistake of my own. After Bianca had been rung up by the local nursery and offered a place, I was concerned that Gemma had heard nothing. When I contacted them they told me that, according to the form I had filled in, Gemma was not yet old enough. It transpired that I had put down her date of birth as '30/11/84' instead of '30/11/83', so they thought she was only two and half instead of three and a half. When I explained the error, they urged me to come along after nursery began and they would see if they could squeeze her in. In the meantime Gemma never tired of telling anyone who would listen precisely how stupid her Mam had been.

When Gemma and I turned up a week later, the headmistress suggested that a place could be found for her with Bianca. The headmistress already knew about Gemma's condition, but when I told her that we had to be very careful about measles, chicken pox and similar illnesses because they could be fatal, she looked surprised. When I further suggested that the nursery should tell me when any of the children caught these infections, so that I could keep Gemma at home, she looked distinctly unhappy. She said she would discuss the matter with the school governors and get back to me as soon as possible.

A few days later she phoned, and Steven answered. She told him that the nursery did not think it was fair to ask the other parents to inform us whenever their children were ill. If this was not acceptable, then Gemma should not attend. As Steven relayed this to me, I thought he was joking. When I realised he was serious, I rang the nursery in a fury. The headmistress confirmed, apparently without emotion, that she did not think other parents should bear that kind of responsibility. I replaced the phone angrily, insisting that she had not heard the last of this. It was almost as if Gemma was putting all the other children at risk, instead of vice versa.

I took the problem to Dr Kernahan in Newcastle. Her aim was to try to give child leukaemia victims as normal a life as possible and she regarded the nursery's action as ridiculous. She promised to contact the headmistress, who subsequently rang me. Sounding a little frosty, she explained that she had changed her mind and would like Gemma to start nursery in October, after half-term. She was preparing a newsletter to be distributed to all the parents, requesting them to notify the school if there were any illnesses in the family. 'Is that OK with you?' she asked me.

My answer not only surprised her, but rather astonished me. 'Well, to tell you the truth I wouldn't feel safe with Gemma in your school because of your previous attitude,' I heard myself saying. 'So thanks but no thanks. Gemma will not be attending your nursery school.'

She protested, but I insisted that that was how I felt. I was not going to make any compromises with my daughter's life. After I hung up, it took me a while to calm down. Then I began to feel terribly guilty, as if I had done something perverse or selfish. I knew how much Gemma wanted to go to nursery, so I did not say anything to her. That evening, when I told Steven what I had done, I expected him to get mad at me. But he basically felt the same, saying he would not feel comfortable with Gemma in the care of people who had initially rejected her. In any case, she would be starting full-time school within a year.

The battle over the attendance allowance started with me filling in forms for the Department of Social Security and informing Dr Kernahan. After three weeks, a doctor came round to assess my application while Gemma was taking a morning nap on the sofa. He asked a series of questions about her condition and the precautions we had to take. He took lots of notes and said we should hear something in a couple of weeks. He did not seem particularly sympathetic.

The attendance allowance board rejected our application, but did not give any detailed reasons. I appealed, and another doctor came round to reassess us. He again asked lots of questions, examined Gemma and took notes. He seemed a little more sympathetic than his predecessor. He was from Seascale, the small village next to Sellafield which had the highest rate of childhood leukaemia. A few weeks later a brown official-looking envelope dropped through the door, telling me that my appeal had been successful and that back-dated attendance allowance at a rate of about £25 a week had been granted.

I was thrilled, but also angry that I had been forced to fight for my rights. If, like many other people, I had not bothered to appeal, I would have got nothing. I was learning that in this life you have to fight for everything. I did not know that the big fights were still to come.

Chapter 6

Who Wants to Live for Ever?

Gemma and Richenda once went on holiday with my parents to a Butlin's camp, where they learned by heart a song that reduced Steven and me to hysterics. They used to perform it for us in the living room, accompanied by graphic hand actions.

> I found myself a baby bumble bee.
> Won't my mother be pleased with me?
> I'm squashing up the baby bumble bee.
> Won't my mother be pleased with me?
> I'm licking up the baby bumble bee.
> Oh, it has just stung me.
> I'm throwing up the baby bumble bee.
> Won't my mother be cross with me?

They had obviously had such an enjoyable time that Steven and I had felt jealous that we had not been there. Another Butlin's holiday was one of our family fantasies, but we never had enough money.

One day Tina slyly asked me what I would most like to give Gemma if money was no object. I told her it would have to be a family holiday in Butlin's that we could always remember. Tina did not at first let on what she was thinking. I learned later that she contacted a mutual acquaintance who worked for Balfour Beatty at Sellafield, Norma Slater, and asked her about organising a collection to send Gemma on holiday. Norma started the ball rolling and, amazingly, people started giving money. Sellafield workers, both those who worked for British Nuclear Fuels and those who were employed by contractors, were very generous. Some of them knew Steven, of course, and others responded to a poster of Gemma. 'Little Gemma D'Arcy is four years old and is dying of leukaemia. Please give generously to send her on a holiday,' it said.

The first phone call I got from Norma Slater told me to plan for a two-week holiday in Butlin's. The second call said that Butlin's was off. 'Never mind. It doesn't matter. At least you tried,' I said.

'Susan, have you got passports?' responded Norma. 'If not, get them – because instead of Butlin's you are going to Disneyworld in Florida.' I was stunned and – uncharacteristically – speechless. The response to the appeal was overwhelming. As well as countless cash donations, one local pub held a fancy dress evening and another a sponsored pub crawl. A young woman from Workington organised a 13-mile sponsored walk, and four Cleator Moor footballers went for an ice-cold dip in the Irish Sea. My friend Helen held a charity night in our local club, at which two singers, Steve Falcon and Tony Kane, gave their services free of charge. Steve Falcon had himself fought and won a battle against cancer, though he lost a leg in the process. He sang Nat King Cole's 'When I Fall in Love', which became the anthem for Gemma's fund-raising campaign:

> In a restless world like this is
> Life is over before it's begun
> And too many moonlight kisses
> Seem to cool in the warmth of the sun.

After the show I went to thank him personally and showed him photos of Gemma. I learned later that he then took it upon himself to raise more money.

The local newspaper and television station got hold of the story and came and interviewed us. It was our first experience of the media and it was a very happy one. The way they presented Gemma's plight was lovely, and made an enormous boost to the fund-raising. Over £10,000 was eventually raised – enough for all four of us to spend a month in Florida, all expenses paid plus spending money. I could not believe how lucky we were: going to Disneyworld was really like a dream come true. I was so grateful to all my friends and all those I did not know who had helped. Gemma was over the moon when we told her. 'Will we meet Mickey Mouse?' she demanded to know.

Unfortunately there were some who were not so happy. After a couple of months of fund-raising, a woman I had got to know from the local branch of the Leukaemia Research Fund called round. Her daughter had previously died of leukaemia. Gemma told her excitedly that she was going to see Mickey Mouse. 'I know you are. That's great,' she said in a forced voice. Knowing that we were not well off, she gave me a pair of shoes for the children. Then she showed me a letter from fourteen members of West Cumbria Leukaemia Research that was due to be published in the local evening newspaper in a couple of days. 'I wanted to show you this before you read it in the paper, so you would not be too shocked,' she said as she left. 'But I am not going to say I am sorry, because I am not.'

Put bluntly, the letter seemed to me to be an appeal to donate money to the Leukaemia Research Fund instead of towards a holiday for Gemma. Published in the *West Cumbrian Evening News and Star*, this is what it said:

> We at West Cumbria Leukaemia Research, more than any, understand the generosity of West Cumbrians who have been touched by the plight of little Gemma D'Arcy. Their generous hearts only want to give, to make up for the rotten luck this family has suffered in being touched by this dreadful disease, leukaemia.
>
> But we do want to point out that there are other children in West Cumbria with leukaemia, whose parents know full well that they may die at any moment, even those who are apparently doing well at the moment. Several children have also recently died of leukaemia . . . Of all those diagnosed in the last four years we have not yet seen one child given the all-clear, and only one has survived to the end of his course of treatment . . .
>
> The reason we are writing is to ask people not to forget that, while it is lovely to send one little girl and her family on holiday,

> there is also an urgent need for money to pay for research and for the bone marrow registers . . . We have taken a noticeable drop in our voluntary donations over the last few months, and appeal to those concerned about leukaemia to help us where they can. After all, you never know whose family is next.

I was upset and angry. When I showed Steven the letter he was furious. He pointed out that people had chosen to give Gemma a holiday rather than donate to the Leukaemia Research Fund in the knowledge that she was unlikely to live long enough to see a cure. I felt as if life was immensely unfair. Just as something extraordinarily good had come along to cheer us up, someone had turned up and knocked the legs from under us. I tried to shrug it off, but it hurt, especially on the day that the newspaper hit the streets.

Thankfully, there were people who still wanted to help Gemma live as fulfilled a life as possible in the short time that might have been left to her – regardless of the leukaemia organisation's advice. A woman from the local hat factory, Kangol Wear, rang and explained that she wanted to hold a collection to buy a present for Gemma. She spoke to Gemma, who said she wanted a new bike with stabilisers. Much to my surprise and Gemma's delight, a brand-new blue bike was delivered within the next few days. Beaming with joy, Gemma rode it around the kitchen, putting in the front basket a brown fluffy teddy that she had also been given. She wanted to take the bike to bed with her, but we managed to agree on just the teddy. A photographer from the newspaper came round and took a nice picture of her on her bike, which in due course appeared on the front page. We still have a home video of Steven and me endlessly trying to teach her to ride the bike in the street, which ends with her falling and hurting her hand.

For Gemma's fourth birthday, on 30 November 1987, we teamed up with Helen, whose daughter Kerry had a birthday around the same time, to organise a double celebration. We hired a magician and a disco, and invited forty children to fill a local hall. There was also a bar for the grown-ups. Gemma was showered with presents, stuffed herself with birthday cake and danced away the afternoon. It was lovely to see her enjoying herself, but I could not help wondering how many more birthdays she would live to see. When Gemma went to bed that night, I could not stop crying. Steven talked about the prospect of Christmas and Disneyland in the spring, but all I could see was death. As I often did, I sat up late at night turning over and over in my mind what had happened to us. Again I tried to think what I could have done to have brought such a tragedy on my family. I thought more and more about Sellafield, its leaking radioactivity and whether it might be to blame. Steven still remained doubtful.

Christmas that year was great. On Christmas Eve Gemma insisted on leaving a mince pie and some milk out for Santa Claus instead of a glass of sherry, because she thought Santa should not drink and drive – a decision which Steven had to accept with good grace. We bought Gemma a toy pram and Richenda a new bike, as she had been jealous of Gemma's ever since it had arrived. We put the bike in the kitchen and sent Richenda in there on Christmas morning on a pretext. She came out looking shocked because she could not at first figure out why it was there. When Tina rang up, Gemma told her that Richenda looked like she was going to pass out. As usual we spent most of Christmas Day with Tina and my father, and Boxing Day with Steven's parents.

In the first two months of 1988 Gemma's bone marrow continued to improve, presumably because we had stopped the busulphan. Before we were due to go to Florida in March, we took her to see Dr Kernahan in Newcastle for a final check-up to make sure she was fit enough to travel. To take with us she gave us a letter which explained precisely what was wrong with Gemma, plus a list of all the possible telephone numbers we could want. She told us that Gemma's blood count was fine, and wished us a wonderful time.

Tina and my mother were at Manchester Airport to see us off. We were a little nervous of flying as I had only flown once, to Italy, while Steven and the children had never set foot in an aeroplane before. As we were all sitting watching planes take off and land, waiting for our flight to be called, Tina slipped away. When I asked her where she had been, her reply was devious: 'Nowhere, just looking about.'

I suspected something was afoot a few minutes later, when she was hailed over the public intercom. She and my mother led the rest of us to Passport Control, where there was a uniformed lady waiting for us holding two airport teddy bears.

'Follow me,' she said briskly, as she gave Gemma and Richenda the teddies. All of us, including Tina and my mother, walked along the corridor and down some steps, ending up on the tarmac in front of the plane. The whole crew was there to meet us. The captain shook hands with Steven and talked to Gemma, and we took lots of photos. We waved goodbye to Tina and my mother on the tarmac as we climbed the steps into the plane, the first to board. The journey, which started with the children crying because of sore ears and ended with them fast asleep, took nine and a half hours in all. When we arrived in Florida it was one o'clock in the morning and the temperature was well over 70° Fahrenheit.

We spent the first week at a plush hotel overlooking the Gulf of Mexico. It was beautiful, although we felt cheated by the beach which was not sandy as it appeared in the brochure, but made up of tiny crushed shells that cut your feet. When the sun went down we would stand on our balcony and watch pelicans swooping down to snatch fish from the sea. That was amazing. Then we drove to our second hotel, where we had a suite of rooms to ourselves and two swimming pools. The first thing we did when we visited Disneyworld was to catch a ferry to the Magic Kingdom, watching Donald Duck and Goofy skiing on the lake. Gemma laughed when Goofy fell in the water. In the Kingdom we queued for more than half an hour – a relatively short time in Disneyworld – so that Gemma could ride Dumbo, the elephant with the huge ears. Gemma got quite mad at the pensioner couple in front of us. 'They're too old for this – it's not fair,' she complained.

Disneyworld was fantastic, but rather wearing after a while. We did not get all around it in a day and decided to save up some of our tickets for a return visit. We spent several days just lounging by the hotel swimming pools, where the girls had made friends. I loved being in a completely new environment where nobody knew about Gemma's condition. It felt wonderfully relaxing, and it was a genuine pleasure watching Gemma and Richenda blossom.

One evening, about halfway through the holiday, I was helping Gemma get dry after a shower when I noticed that her legs and arms were absolutely covered in bruises – not just two or three, but scores of them all over, each the size of an old penny. Gemma said they did not hurt, but we decided we had better ring Dr Kernahan in Newcastle to ask her advice. We were worried that Gemma's bone marrow was collapsing again. When we had worked out the time difference and dialled the number we got straight through. Dr Kernahan thought that we ought to get Gemma's blood tested as soon as possible, and telephone her with the results.

Early the next morning we drove to the nearest medical centre, explained what we needed and handed over Dr Kernahan's letter. Gemma was disappointed that we were in a hospital, not a shopping mall. I told her that although she was on holiday her leukaemia was not, so she had to have another blood test. We had hardly had time to inspect the centre's plush surroundings before a female doctor in a white coat advanced to meet us. She introduced herself and queried exactly what we wanted. At first she did not believe that Gemma had chronic myeloid leukaemia, because it was so rare in America. But I convinced her it was true and she agreed to take some blood.

As she prepared the needles, Gemma started screaming at the top of her voice. The doctor asked the nurse to bring in what she called a 'tommy board', which I assumed was some kind of toy. It turned out to be the child's equivalent of a straitjacket, a series of straps on a board designed to pin down flailing arms and legs. I refused to let such a device be used on my child. I grabbed Gemma's hand firmly, and presented it to the doctor so that she could take some blood. I was angry with both of them.

When the doctor suggested that, because of holidays, it could take a week before the results of the analysis were ready, I lost my temper, saying that we would not have bothered to come if we had known it would take so long. The doctor pointed out that a delay might not matter as we might not be able to fly back to Britain in any case – if Gemma's blood count turned out to be low she would not advise air travel, because of the risk of her eardrums bursting and causing her to bleed to death. I argued that that was further reason to know the results as soon as possible so that we could make alternative arrangements to get home. Eventually she promised to do what she could. On the way out, we had to pay $50 at the receptionist's till. We did not have any medical insurance, as no one would provide cover for a child with a fatal disease. It felt like leaving a supermarket, not a medical centre.

The next two days were full of anxiety while we waited for the results. We were afraid to spend any money in case we had to buy new tickets home, or pay for private treatment in America. When I telephoned the doctor, she said she had just received the results and read them out. Gemma's red blood cell count was 10.5, her white cell count 6 and her platelet count 200. I knew enough now to be sure that this meant that Gemma was all right – a verdict that was confirmed by Dr Kernahan when I telephoned her. The American doctor suggested that Gemma's bruising could have been caused by her constantly getting in and out of the hotel swimming pool.

After the scare, we all thoroughly enjoyed what was left of our holiday. We paid a return visit to Disneyworld, where Gemma and Richenda had their pictures taken with Mickey Mouse. We visited bush gardens where there were alligators and snakes. The children got a ride on an elephant, which they said they would never forget. In the last week, by which time we were quite looking forward to coming home, we went on a shopping spree. We spoiled the kids rotten, buying them virtually anything they wanted, as well as lots of presents for friends and relatives back home.

The flight home was terrible. We hit turbulence and for about an hour the plane felt as if it was constantly dropping out of the sky. A much-travelled fellow passenger, who started off by boasting how safe aeroplanes were, swore that she would never fly again. Thankfully Steven and the children slept through the whole ordeal. I was particularly anxious, because I had had this feeling in Florida that I was pregnant again. I had mentioned it to Steven and the children, who had been really pleased and already started arguing about names. When we finally got home, tired but glad to be back,

I had this strange but powerful sense of security surrounding me and Gemma. With another child starting to grow inside me, there was hope: a new brother or sister for Richenda and – perhaps – a new life for Gemma.

As my pregnancy progressed, I started to feel ill. I lost weight and felt physically sick most of the time. I began to worry that it might go wrong. At fifteen weeks, I had an amniocentesis to check whether the foetus had any severe disabilities like spina bifida or Down's syndrome. It was a great relief when the results came back negative. I was disappointed, though, when I learned it was another girl, as I would have preferred a boy for a change, but I soon got over that. Our consultant, Dr Jenny Kernahan, was very pleased for us and told me all about the bone marrow tests that could be carried out when the baby was ten to twelve months old. All of us were looking forward optimistically to the birth, buying tiny little vests and dresses whenever we went to the shops. Gemma and Richenda even managed to resolve their argument over the baby's name: she was to be called Janine.

One morning I felt much sicker than usual. I noticed a few specks of blood on my sheets, so tried to take it easy until the midwife came in the afternoon. She told me to put my feet up and said she would try and arrange for a doctor to call later the same day. But it was not until nine o'clock the following morning that I eventually received a telephone call from the doctor's surgery asking if I could come in within half an hour. By that time I had begun to wonder whether I had been over-reacting, although I agreed to attend. After a urine test and an internal examination, the doctor told me that everything seemed fine. I was so relieved that I burst into tears when I came out of the surgery.

But at home later, I still felt awful. Richenda was staying at Tina's that night and, after Gemma had gone to bed, I sat and watched television with Steven. Suddenly I felt a very sharp pain in my stomach. Because of what the doctor had said, I tried to ignore it, hoping it would go away. Stephen was not very sympathetic either, suspecting me of crying wolf. After he had gone to bed I was worried that I would not be able to sleep, so I stayed up and made some tea.

The pains, which felt very different from labour, were getting worse. I telephoned the emergency call-out service and another doctor came to see me at about one o'clock in the morning. Despite what I told her about my urine test the previous day, she thought I had a water infection. I said I thought I was dilating, like in the initial stages of labour. But she gave me some antibiotics and two sleeping tablets and told me to go to bed. I took the tablets and tried to sleep with Steven, who had woken up and asked what all the fuss was about. But I was tossing and turning so much that I decided to move to the sofa so as not to disturb him. He had to go to work early in the morning.

At around three o'clock, still unable to sleep because of the increasing pains, I telephoned the maternity ward of the local hospital. A nurse asked me whether it was my first baby and, for the first time, I felt I was being taken seriously. She promised to send an ambulance at once. I woke up Steven, who was not very happy, and telephoned Tina, whose husband, Russell, came round quickly to collect Gemma, who slept through the entire drama. Steven accompanied me to the hospital, where a doctor told me I was four centimetres dilated. 'Mrs D'Arcy, I'm afraid your baby is going to be born today,' he told me. 'You do realise that, as you are only twenty-four weeks pregnant, the baby might not survive.'

I was given an injection to ease the pain, and slept a little while. When I woke, Steven was sitting at my side, brimful of apologies. He said that he had not believed me because a nurse and two doctors had said I was all right. He was upset, and admitted he should have known better. Distressed as I was, my response was cruel. 'Do you believe me now?' I kept yelling at him as I was giving birth. The doctors said it should be a short labour, but unfortunately it lasted seventeen hours. A paediatrician was present during the final stages to try and save Janine, but he could not. Her umbilical cord, wrapped around her neck, strangled her before she breathed a single breath of life.

Later I was asked if I would like to see her. I refused at first, my head full of worries about how I was going to tell Gemma and Richenda. One of the midwives brought me a Polaroid photograph of her. She looked lovely – a little like Gemma but with Richenda's colours. When Tina came to see me, we were asked again if we would like to see her body. I still refused, but after Tina and Steven said they would like to, I changed my mind. When the nurse handed her to me wrapped in a blanket, she looked so tiny and so innocent. She still had webbed hands and feet, but she was all there. I studied her features and gave her to Steven and then Tina to hold. We were all scared and upset, because we had never held a dead child before.

That night I could not stop crying. I kept wondering what the hospital were going to do with her now. Would they incinerate her, put her in a rubbish bin, or bury her? A nurse told me that she would be cremated with a priest in attendance saying a prayer, and that helped me settle down after a while. Steven told Gemma and Richenda, but I was still worried about how they would react when I came home. In the event, Richenda made me a cup of tea and Gemma put her arms around me. 'It's nice to have you home, Mam,' she said, squeezing my neck.

I was surprised that at first they avoided asking me about Janine. Eventually I asked if they would like to see some photographs of her. They grabbed them from me and examined them carefully. They started squabbling over which of them she resembled. I suggested that she had a bit of both of them – Gemma's nose and Richenda's dark skin. They seemed pleased with that idea and sat with the photographs for over an hour, ignoring me. Gradually, I suppose, we all came to terms with the enormity of what we had lost: a sister, a daughter and a new chance for Gemma.

On our next visit to Newcastle, Dr Kernahan examined Gemma as usual and announced that her bone marrow had recovered sufficiently for us start the busulphan tablets again. This time she suggested gradually building up the dose in order to reduce the risk of another bone marrow collapse. Then she made an unexpected proposal: would we be willing to help the British Bone Marrow Donor Appeal? This was an organisation that had been founded in 1987 by Malcolm Thomas after his ten-year-old daughter, Alexandra, died of leukaemia. He searched every bone marrow register in the world to try and save his daughter's life, but was not able to find a suitable

Gemma at thirteen
months old in the park
at St Bees beach.

Gemma, 'the milk bottle',
at two years old.

Gemma in August 1987, one month after she was diagnosed as having leukaemia.

Gemma and Bianca's Christening.

On the runway before our trip to Disneyland in March 1988. *Back row:* Russell, Steven, Tina, Susan, Nina; *front row:* Nikki, Richenda, Gemma, Bianca and my mother, Nana Pat.

Sunshine and smiles for Gemma in Florida.

Gemma's first and last school photograph.

Dying but not ill. Gemma at five years old and on the busulphan treatment.

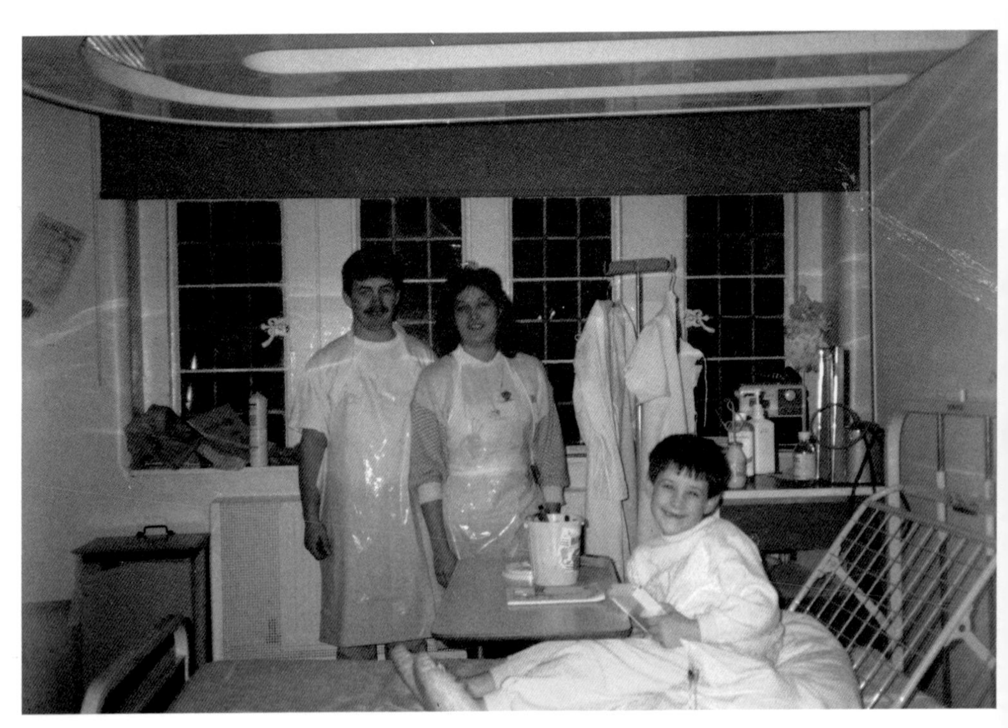

Tina and Russell with Gemma at the hospital – this was the beginning of her no-turning-back treatment. Note the air flow at the top of the picture.

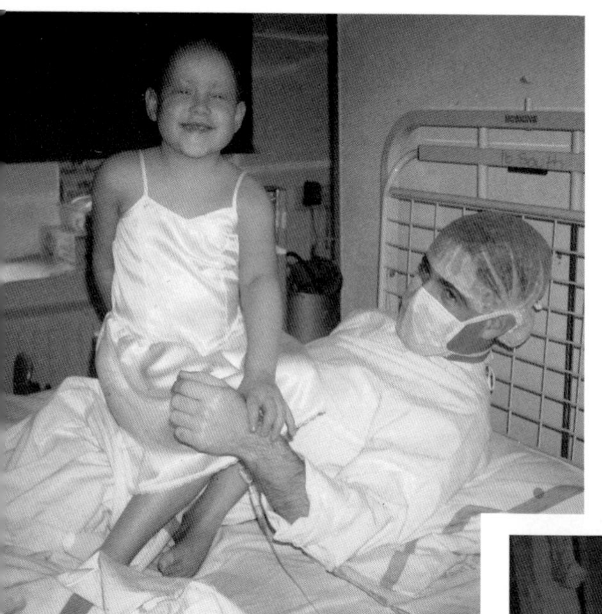

Steve giving Gemma a cuddle as best he could.

This was the third and final bone marrow transplant. They say that if you want something done properly you should do it youself, and that's just what Gemma did!

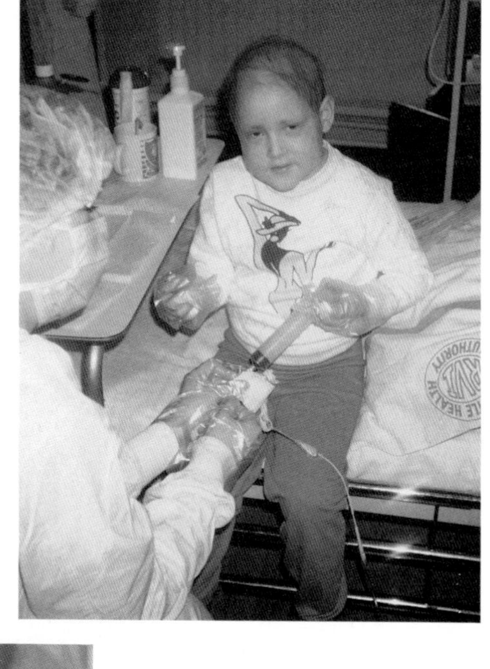

Gemma ripping up the red boundary tape.

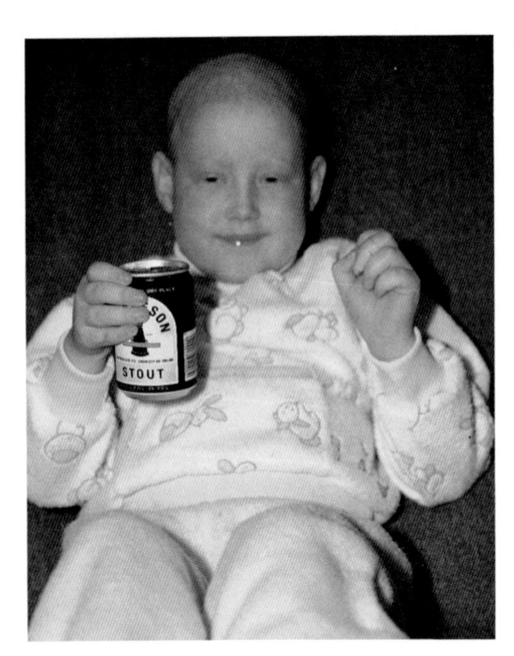

Gemma with her favourite
medicine – a can of
Mackeson Stout!

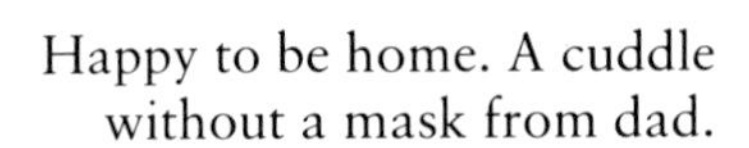

Happy to be home. A cuddle
without a mask from dad.

At the funfair just two weeks
before Gemma died.

Me and Steve with Samina at her Christening.

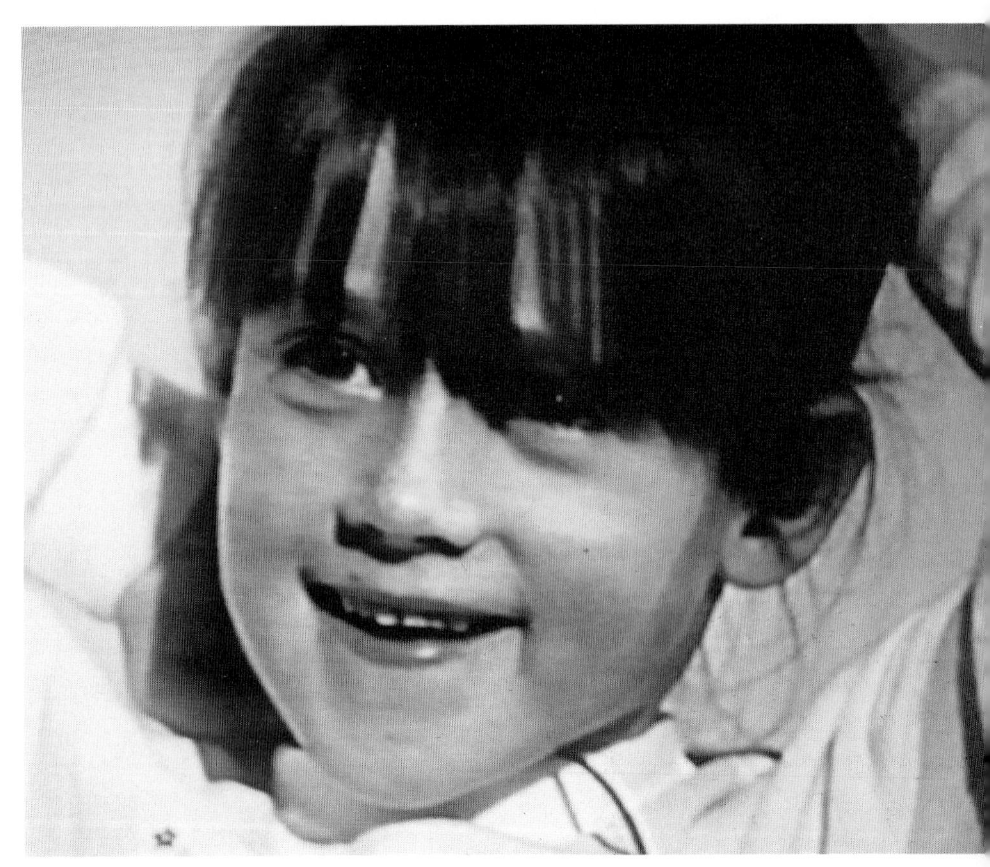

Gemma Donna Louise D'Arcy.

donor in time. He received notification of a possible match just a few days after Alexandra's death. After that he decided to dedicate his life to improving the system so that other people would not have to endure similar tragedies.

There were several problems with the way the existing register operated. For a start, there were not enough people listed as potential bone marrow donors because relatively few knew about it, which obviously decreased the likelihood of matches being found for victims. Because there were so many different types of bone marrow and the analysis of tissue types was so difficult, the process of searching for potential donors was very laborious, time-consuming and expensive. Malcolm Thomas was campaigning for a comprehensive, computerised system, in which everyone who gave blood at one of the British Blood Transfusion Service's centres would be asked if they were willing to become a bone marrow donor. This would greatly boost the number of donors and speed up the process of finding potential matches – but it would inevitably cost a great deal of money. The British Bone Marrow Donor Appeal was asking for £5 million to help establish a register of a hundred thousand donors.

Steven and I agreed without hesitation to do whatever we could to help. Gemma was in precisely the same position as Alexandra had been. Because her type of bone marrow was so rare, we had so far been unable to find her a matching donor and, unless we did, she would die. We agreed to get Gemma's photograph taken for some publicity leaflets, although we had no idea at the time just how much publicity it would generate. A picture of Gemma appeared on the front of the appeal's leaflet under the headline 'Will you help to save my life?' Underneath it said: 'My name is Gemma and I have leukaemia. I want to live and I need your help.' Inside it quoted me talking about the agony of waiting when time was running out, and described another case of a little boy who was equally desperate for a donor. It made quite an impact locally and nationally.

Malcolm Thomas, who personally did everything he could to find a donor for Gemma, asked both of us to go to Newcastle when the leaflet was published and give a television interview. Gemma and

I sat beside each other and, when the interviewer asked me what would happen without a bone marrow transplant, Gemma butted in and told everyone that she would die. If she did get a transplant, she said, she would be able to catch chicken pox and measles. When it was broadcast the interview affected a lot of people and brought many donations to the appeal, with which we were honoured to be associated. Malcolm Thomas also persuaded Brian May from the rock group Queen to help record a special fund-raising version of the old Queen song 'Who Wants to Live for Ever?', which Gemma thought was lovely. She used to sing along to it.

During our work for the appeal we were privileged to meet Denise Morse, an adult victim of leukaemia whose last few months of life were the subject of an intensely moving television documentary. She first became famous when she took part in a television chat show with Terry Wogan, talking about how she needed a bone marrow transplant to save her life and how she was facing the prospect of death with the aid of her religion. She described how her family were planning to celebrate Christmas several months early because she was not expected to live until 25 December. She wanted to see the joy on her three children's faces one more time before she died.

Steven and I met Denise at a press conference where we were all appealing for funds for the bone marrow register. She was very ill and very weak. She had to wear a face mask all the time to protect her against infections, as her immune system had been badly damaged. When the press conference was over, we sat and talked for a short while. Before she left, she gave Gemma a hug and a kiss and put her arms around Steven. 'Don't be afraid to let Gemma die,' she whispered in his ear. 'I will be waiting at the gates of heaven for her.'

Chapter 7

Satan in the House

The advertisement cost £94.50 and appeared in the *Whitehaven News* on Thursday, 28 July 1988. It was headed 'Leukaemia: Legal Test Cases', and read:

> Official surveys have demonstrated that there is a significant excess of leukaemia amongst children living in the vicinity of the Sellafield and Dounreay nuclear processing plants. Scientific opinion now accepts that there may well be a link between the leukaemias and the nuclear plants.
>
> Under the Nuclear Installation Act, British Nuclear Fuels are statutorily required to compensate any individual who has suffered injury as a result of their operations. We believe that there may now be sufficient scientific evidence to persuade the courts in this country that some leukaemias are caused by the action of British Nuclear Fuels, which would enable the victims to be compensated.
>
> Our firm is experienced in dealing with radiation cases and has been involved in a number of cases against British Nuclear Fuels and the United Kingdom Atomic Energy Authority. We ensure that, wherever possible, our clients are financially protected by a Legal Aid certificate.
>
> If your child suffered or is still suffering from leukaemia, if you live in the surrounding area of Sellafield and if you are interested in making a claim against British Nuclear Fuels, then why not telephone us. Your case will be treated in absolute confidence.

I first heard of the advertisement the day before it appeared. A reporter from the *Whitehaven News* rang me when I was in the middle of bad-temperedly tidying up the house. He told me what the advertisement was going to say and asked what I thought about it. I'm afraid I was rather rude, taking him to task for suggesting that I should know anything about it before it had even been published. When he asked whether I would be responding, I said it was none of his business. 'What did you say the lawyer's name was?' I asked before I hung up.

As I continued washing the dishes and vacuuming the floor, I could not get the name out of my head: Martyn Day. On impulse I picked up the telephone and rang Directory Enquiries. They could not find a lawyer's number in that name, but gave me the number of a firm of solicitors called Leigh, Day & Co. in London. I wrote it down, left it by the telephone and went back to the cleaning. When I had finished and made myself a cup of tea, I sat thinking about what to do. Although I had long brooded over the possibility that radioactivity from Sellafield was implicated in Gemma's suffering, I had done nothing about it other than talk. As with any major decision, I dithered, trying to sort out the pros and cons in my mind. Would it be worth it? Would Steven be angry? What about the rest of the family and my friends? Crucially, would it help Gemma? I really did not know the answers, but I was excited by the idea of legal action. 'What the hell, there's nothing to lose,' I thought finally, and picked up the telephone again.

As soon as I told the receptionist that I was the mother of a child leukaemia victim near Sellafield, I was put through to Martyn Day. Speaking with an educated, friendly accent, he asked about Gemma. He invited me to a meeting of the local leukaemia research group which he was attending in a few days' time. I refused because of my dispute with the group over fund-raising for Gemma and because I wanted a private meeting with him. He agreed to come and see me at home the following Sunday.

Afterwards I was filled with doubts. I was particularly worried about what Steven would say, knowing that he was still refusing to accept that Sellafield could be to blame. The first person I told was

Tina, who thought I should listen to what Martyn Day had to say and then decide. Steven's reaction, over bought-in chips and beer that evening, was irate. He said that no one would ever prove a connection between Sellafield and leukaemia, and that BNFL was far too big a company for a family like ours to take on. 'Are you cracked?' he demanded. 'I work there. They pay my wages, clothe and feed us. What evidence is there that they have caused Gemma's illness? This so-called solicitor is only out to make money for himself.'

I pointed out that Martyn Day was just offering to prove or disprove what I had been suspecting, and begged Steven to listen to what he had to say. He reluctantly agreed, but insisted that he did not have to accept it, or even have to be pleasant to him. I also asked Tina and Russell to be present so that we could all decide what to do together. I tried to explain simply to Gemma and Richenda what was happening.

The first I saw of Martyn Day was through the curtain on our glass back door. He looked very official, wearing a suit and tie and carrying a small briefcase under his arm. He came through to the kitchen where we plonked him down on a chair at the table. There he faced what he later described as the 'D'Arcy mafia': Tina and I at the table, Steven and Russell standing. I think he was more nervous than we were. 'I realised that I was genuinely being put on my mettle and that there would be no easy ride in this house,' he said later.

I launched the interview by asking how on earth he expected to succeed in a claim against BNFL. He went over the scientific and legal backgrounds, explaining about the local leukaemia cluster, the extent of Sellafield's radioactive pollution and the occupational risks faced by workers. We kept stopping him and asking questions. We were particularly worried about how any legal action would be financed, as it would undoubtedly cost a large amount of money. Martyn explained about the Legal Aid process and how we would have to apply for money from the government. Although there would obviously be difficulties in persuading them to fund an action against a government-owned company like BNFL, he thought that we would have a reasonable chance. He said he had already been contacted by twenty-five families locally as a result of the advertisement in the *Whitehaven News* – a number that later rose to forty.

We explained in turn about Gemma's illness and her prognosis. Martyn asked a lot of questions about my previous jobs and Steven's work at Sellafield. He asked about our visits to the beaches near Sellafield. After a substantial interchange of information, during which Martyn must have realised that there was a disagreement within the family, he told us that he thought we had a very strong case. But he warned us that a legal action would bring no instant results and could, with appeals, stretch over five or ten years. We went into another room to discuss our response in private, leaving him with Gemma. She talked to him in her usual matter-of-fact manner about her leukaemia, which she defined as 'bad blood', and how it made her special. She told him how she needed a bone marrow transplant so that she could catch chicken pox and measles like other children.

In the next room, Steven and I slugged it out. It was obvious that I had already made up my mind in favour of pursuing a claim, and he told me in no uncertain terms that I was making a big mistake. He argued that we had nothing to gain from a court action, whereas Martyn stood to gain a great deal in terms of finance and reputation. I said that I did not really care what Martyn's motives were, but I had come to believe that Sellafield was the cause of cancers in the area. Now that my daughter was dying from a form of cancer, I felt that I had to stand up and shout about it. If we won the case, it would not only provide Gemma with some much-needed money, but could also force BNFL to clean up their act and prevent other families from losing children. 'We should not have to suffer so that other people can make profits,' I said angrily. 'That man in there is going to give me a chance, not just to point my finger but hopefully to prove what is going on in this area. Or at least to try.'

Tina agreed with me, saying that the link between Sellafield and cancers was something that we had discussed and long suspected. She pointed out that if we could find the cause, we would be nearer to finding a cure. Russell, the only one of us who was a born and bred Cumbrian, had not said much until then. Tina asked what he thought and we all turned towards him, as if he had the deciding vote. 'Go for it,' he said. Steven, realising he was out-voted, complained that what he thought did not matter. I told him that it did. He himself did not have to get involved in the legal action – all I was asking was that he would not stand in my way. On the basis that he would be kept out of it, he agreed.

Martyn was very pleased when we went through to tell him the news. He understood Steven's wish not to be connected with the case, but pointed out that he would have to sign some forms, which Steven accepted. Martyn got out the Legal Aid application form for us to sign and promised to keep in touch. He later wrote about our first meeting, saying it left him emotionally drained. He described how he went and lay on a grassy bank overlooking Derwentwater near Keswick in the late afternoon sunshine, thinking how desperately sad it was that all our suffering could have been man-made. 'If I needed any further persuasion that my decision to take on BNFL was correct, that afternoon provided it,' he said.

> Gemma was one of the most beautiful young girls that I had ever come across. With her strong Cumbrian accent and her hair in plaits, she had a mixture of vivaciousness and chattiness that was very, very endearing. It was a real pleasure for me to become known by her as her lawyer, which was how she would continually refer to me. I felt it a privilege to be able to act for her and I have had few clients in my working life whose plight has affected me so deeply.

My next task was to tell the rest of the family before they read anything about it in the newspapers. My father, although he was very worried about the difficulties we would face, was supportive. I promised him that I would give up the case if he wanted me to, but he urged me to keep at it as there was 'definitely something going on'.

Telling Steven's parents was not so easy, because his father had worked at Sellafield for a long time and was happy in his job there as a quantity surveyor. I chose Sunday afternoon, when we were all sitting down in their living room after the usual delicious three-course lunch with wine. Ged, Steven's father, responded by suggesting that he would arrange for some of BNFL's experts to talk to me about precisely what goes on at Sellafield and to inform me about all the safety measures designed to protect the public from radiation. He thought I ought to be given a guided tour of the plant, and pleaded with me not to do anything irrevocable until I had heard the other side of the story. But I told him I had made up my mind and had already signed the forms applying for Legal Aid. Listening to BNFL's propaganda would not make the slightest difference to my determination to proceed, and we would just have to agree to differ. Steven explained that he disagreed with what I was doing, but could not stand in my way. I then changed the subject and decided it was time for us to leave.

When the children were in bed that evening, Steven took me to task for the different ways in which I had broached the subject with our respective families. Although I had offered my father a veto, I had not even asked his father whether he minded. My view was that our families were bound to be deeply divided on the issue, and there was no point in arguing about it. We each had to concentrate on doing what we believed to be right and best for Gemma.

A couple of weeks after Martyn Day's visit, I was approached by the local media and asked to take part in television and newspaper interviews about the legal action. I was nervous about whether I should agree, and asked Martyn's advice. He thought that it could help let people know what I was doing and why, but the final decision was up to me. I decided that I would talk, partly because people would already be familiar with Gemma and her plight from the earlier interviews I had given. I thought it was very important to keep the legal action distinct from fund-raising for the bone marrow appeal, so that the two issues did not become confused in the public mind. But I again failed to appreciate at the time just how big a story it was going to be.

Steven was not at all pleased. The television company wanted to interview him as well to find out how he felt. I asked him once, but, as I expected, he refused point-blank and I did not ask him again. The television people badgered me to try and persuade him to change his mind, but I would not. When they came to interview me, I sat in the living room with Gemma by my side. The interview seemed to go on for ever, and afterwards they asked if they could film Gemma playing and me washing up. I did not like the idea of women always being portrayed at the kitchen sink, so I suggested they film us both playing instead. When the item was broadcast the following evening, I hid nervously in the kitchen when Steven shouted to tell me we were on. I never liked watching myself on television when other people were around, preferring to watch a recording later on my own. Tina boosted my confidence by saying she thought I came over well. Even Steven thought I had been good. 'But be careful, Susan,' he said. 'Don't let them use you.'

In October 1988 the Legal Aid Board, the body that decides upon Legal Aid applications, wrote to Martyn Day suggesting that we and the other twenty-four families that he was representing were likely to be granted financial assistance. But before we were, in an unprecedented intervention in the Legal Aid process, BNFL authorised its solicitors, Freshfield's of London, to write to the Legal Aid Board requesting that we should be turned down. They argued that our case had no chance of success because it would not be possible to prove that radiation from Sellafield had caused the leukaemias. The legal action would, they claimed, be a complete waste of public money and should be rejected. Martyn, who had never before heard of a potential defendant attempting to prevent the granting of Legal Aid, was outraged. Although BNFL was legally entitled to argue its case, he thought the morality of its action in attempting to cut off our one route of access to justice was dubious. I thought that the company's efforts to stop Legal Aid betrayed its guilt. If it was so sure of its innocence, why was it afraid of arguing it out in open court?

Despite Martyn's submission of further scientific evidence in support of our claim, in February 1989 the Legal Aid Board issued a letter rejecting our applications. Martyn, choked with the injustice of it, rang us first to convey the bad news. Gemma picked up the telephone and, after a short conversation, ran to me shouting: 'We've been turned down, Mam, we've been turned down.' I was beside myself with rage. Without hesitation I told Martyn that we would have to keep on fighting, and he described how we could go about appealing. We had to appeal to the so-called Area Committee, which involved four or five lawyers. We had the right to submit further evidence and could request an oral hearing in person. I said that if it would be helpful, I was quite prepared to appear before the Area Committee myself. That would be highly unusual, Martyn said, but possible.

So it was that, the following month, Gemma and I found ourselves sitting around a huge polished mahogany table in London with about a dozen well-dressed lawyers, arguing our case for Legal Aid. We were represented by Stephen Sedley QC, who had agreed to waive his fees, and supported by Professor Edward Radford, an American radiation expert. Martyn was there, of course, as were a clutch of lawyers representing BNFL and the members of the Area Committee. With Gemma perched on my knee, I felt rather out of place amidst all the suits and ties, and she soon became irritable at having to keep still and quiet for so long. Martyn remembers her crying at one point and me explaining in a whisper that she was over-awed by the occasion: 'She knows it's an important day, but cannot understand why.'

I did not understand much of what was being said either, but when I heard someone suggest that we should wait thirty years for more evidence, I could not contain myself. 'Excuse me,' I butted in. 'Speaking as a mother of a child with leukaemia, my daughter will not be here in thirty years' time and it is her that the Legal Aid is for.' After I had spoken everyone was quiet for a few seconds, and I could feel myself trembling. Then they continued with their arcane debate, exchanging endless legal points as to why our court case should or should not go ahead. After two hours Gemma was relieved to get out of the room. The Area Committee promised a verdict the following day.

The next morning we were invited to appear live on breakfast television with Martyn. Before we went on, Gemma was shown around the studio and even allowed to control the camera while the news was being read – which made the programme producers sweat somewhat! After the interview, which went off well, we travelled back with Martyn to his office to await the crucial telephone call that would reveal the outcome of our appeal. As we sat in the crowded underground train, a woman opposite was staring at us so hard that I began to wonder if she was crazy. But then she suddenly asked whether we had been on television that morning. 'Well, I hope you win your battle, not just for Legal Aid, but for compensation. You deserve to,' she told us.

Gemma was very chuffed, and I was surprised and very pleased that total strangers were offering us their support. It made me feel that I was fighting a decent cause, a cause with which ordinary people throughout the country would sympathise. It was very heartening. As we were walking from the underground station to Martyn's office, Gemma started to complain that her legs were hurting. Martyn, anxious to be in his office in time for the expected telephone call from the Legal Aid Board, hoisted her on to his shoulders. When we arrived, Gemma started playing with one of the office computers and after a short while Martyn took the call. While he was talking we tried to make out what he was being told, but it was impossible. When he had finished, he looked down. 'That was the Legal Aid Board,' he said, and then looked up. 'We've got it.'

The office erupted. I felt like I had just won the pools and Gemma danced about with joy. Martyn later described it as 'one of the most euphoric and triumphant moments of my life'. We held a press conference to announce our victory, and I gave a bewildering series of interviews for radio and television. Press photographers were still hounding Gemma and me as we caught a taxi to the station for the train home. When Steven met us a few hours later at Carlisle, he said that the telephone at home had not stopped ringing with all the local media wanting interviews. Gemma and I had become small-time superstars. I was glad of the opportunity to explain publicly what I was doing and why, because I believed it would help Gemma. I was also keen to say what I thought of BNFL's attempt to deprive us of Legal Aid. The company had made a big mistake in trying to stop me. I was now convinced that it had something to hide.

Later in 1989 another high-profile case that Martyn was taking against BNFL came to the High Court in London. He was representing the Merlin family, who had been forced to sell at a loss their dream house overlooking the Ravenglass estuary because plutonium from Sellafield had been detected in their house dust. Christopher and Christine Merlin were claiming £150,000 compensation for their wrecked lives. They bought the house, Mountain Ash, for £32,750 in 1973 in order to escape from the rat race in the South of England. They first suspected that their home might be contaminated in 1977 when the government's National Radiological Protection Board erected a radiation monitor in their garden to test how much radioactivity was being blown ashore from the sea and mudflats. After the Board refused to monitor inside their house, the Merlins privately arranged with Professor Edward Radford, the former chairman of a US government advisory committee on radiation risks, for the contents of a vacuum cleaner bag to be analysed in America. Concentrations of plutonium were found to be one thousand times greater than the background levels caused by nuclear weapons tests; levels of americium, an equally dangerous radioactive material, were seventeen thousand times greater.

Christopher and Christine, along with their two young boys, Sam and Ben, and their two dogs would often go walking around the Ravenglass estuary. The mud they picked up on their shoes and paws and carried into the house was easily the most radioactively polluted mud in Britain. Not surprisingly, alarmed at the risks to their health, they decided that they had to sell up and move out. But, equally unsurprisingly, nobody wanted to buy Mountain Ash, the pollution of which had been widely reported in the media. In the end the Merlins were forced to auction the house to the highest bidder – a BNFL worker who bought it for £35,500 in 1984. At the time it was professionally valued at £60,000. Unfortunately they lost their court case because the judge, Mr Justice Gatehouse, ruled in April 1990 that the law governing compensation from nuclear plants only helped people who had suffered injury or death. There was no legal provision to compensate people for financial or emotional loss. The law did not mend broken dreams.

The preparation of our claim against BNFL got slowly under way after we had won Legal Aid, occasionally attracting more publicity. Of the forty West Cumbrian families who ended up contacting Martyn Day, he selected four to lead the fight. They were Elizabeth Reay, whose ten-month-old baby daughter, Dorothy, had died of leukaemia in 1962 and whose husband, George, had worked at Sellafield for twenty-eight years; Vivien Hope, who had been left infertile and partially disabled after contracting non-Hodgkin's lymphoma, a very rare disease closely related to leukaemia, and whose father also worked at Sellafield; Jennifer Renwick, whose three-year-old son, Ian, had died of leukaemia in 1971 after drinking milk from a farm next to Sellafield; and Gemma. Whenever I got the opportunity, I told people why I was pursuing BNFL. It was not the money – though of course that would have been useful – it was the over-riding need to ensure that Gemma's suffering was not in vain, that other children would not have to endure what she had to endure.

I did what I could to help in the early stages of the case, until Gemma was admitted to hospital for the traumatic series of events which I will recount in the next chapter. Then I had other more pressing priorities, which I know Martyn understood. He visited Gemma in hospital in January 1990, and left visibly shocked at how ill she had become. But the following month there was one event that did intrude. In shifting the publicity about our claim from the inside of newspapers to the front pages, it opened my eyes to the extraordinary manner in which some sections of the media behave. In ways of which I did not always approve, it changed the whole nature and direction of the legal case. Most unexpectedly of all, by pointing a finger at the fathers of the Sellafield leukaemia victims it totally changed Steven's attitude.

The first inkling I had that something was afoot was when the senior consultant in charge of Gemma's treatment in Newcastle, Dr Alan Craft, took me aside and told me that a report was going to be published the following day linking Sellafield to childhood leukaemia. He did not know all the details, but knew it had been written by a respected colleague of his, Professor Martin Gardner, a medical statistician from Southampton University. It was another of the follow-up reports to Sir Douglas Black's inquiry originally prompted by Yorkshire Television's documentary on Sellafield. Dr Craft thought that the report would help my legal action, but he was worried by the level of media attention it would provoke. He promised he would try to protect Gemma and me from over-enthusiastic reporters on hospital grounds. I phoned home and warned Steven, who was still refusing to talk to the media, about what was going to happen. But again, none of us really anticipated the enormity of the explosion.

Professor Gardner, who headed the Medical Research Council's epidemiological unit at Southampton, had examined 97 cases of cancer, including 52 leukaemias, 22 non-Hodgkin's lymphoma and 23 Hodgkin's lymphoma, in people under the age of twenty-five who had been born in West Cumbria between 1950 and 1985. He confirmed his earlier finding that the rate of childhood leukaemia in Seascale was ten times the national average, but then went a crucial step further. Ten of the 52 leukaemia victims had fathers who worked at Sellafield, many of whom had officially recorded high doses of radiation at work. In his expert opinion there was a clear link between the levels of radiation exposure amongst the fathers and the development of the disease in their children. The risk was greatest for men who, immediately prior to conception, had received total doses of over 100 millisieverts, a measure of radiation dose which reflects the expected impact of different types of radioactivity on living cells. These men were between six and eight times more likely than average to father leukaemic children. Gardner concluded: 'The raised incidence of leukaemia, particularly, and non-Hodgkin's lymphoma among children near Sellafield was associated with paternal employment and recorded whole body-penetrating radiation during working at the plant before conception. The association can explain statistically the observed geographical excess.'

The clear implication of this report, which was published in the

British Medical Journal, was that radiation at lower levels than hitherto expected was somehow damaging fathers' sperm in a way that increased their offspring's susceptibility to leukaemia. It was obviously a tremendous boost to our legal campaign, although I did not understand its full significance until Martyn rang the hospital to tell me. Steven, who had started taking calls from the media at seven o'clock in the morning, decided to take the day off work and join me at Gemma's bedside in Newcastle. The hospital switchboard was inundated with calls from journalists who wanted to talk to us, but we decided that we should do as we had originally intended – spend the time with Gemma. Amongst many others, we refused a request to appear on Robert Kilroy Silk's morning television show *Kilroy*. We were pestered by one besuited breakfast television reporter, who hung around the ward despite the staff's best efforts to get rid of him. He eventually disappeared after Steven threatened to break his neck if he refused to leave us alone.

We eventually left Gemma on the ward at about eleven that night, to return to our room elsewhere in the hospital grounds. On our small portable television we just caught the end of the BBC's *Newsnight* programme, on which they briefly showed the front pages of the following morning's newspapers. We thought we caught a glimpse of Gemma, but could not be sure. When the newspaper trolley came round the ward the following morning we realised that we were on several front pages, including a large picture of Steven and Gemma on the *Times* and another picture of Gemma dominating the front of the *Daily Telegraph*. We were quoted in almost every paper, sometimes saying things that we had never said, although we had declined to give a single interview the previous day. Some reports suggested that Gemma was in a coma. When I looked up from my reading, she was sitting up in bed happily completing a jigsaw puzzle.

Throughout the day, as Steven read and digested the reports, the implication of what Professor Gardner was saying began to sink in. Back in our room after Gemma had settled down for the night, he wept. 'I've done that to Gemma. I put her in here all because I worked at that place. If she dies it will be my fault,' he said angrily. I tried to comfort him by insisting that the blame was not his but BNFL's. It was BNFL that should have warned him of the risks he was taking, because he had no way of knowing. 'I've never been behind you in this legal action before,' he told me, 'but now I want you to fight all the way. Phone Martyn and tell him to get the bastards. My little girl is dying because of them.'

Back in Cleator Moor, my sister Tina did not escape the media attention. One reporter from the *News of the World* had knocked on my neighbours' doors and been directed to her. He told her that the newspaper was prepared to offer £3,000 for an exclusive interview with Steven. Tina phoned me at the hospital to ask what I thought. Angered by the idea that the reporter had been snooping around asking questions, I refused, saying that £3,000 was not enough. To my amazement, he immediately upped his offer to £5,000, which Steven and I, ever desperate for cash, accepted. I immediately felt guilty about taking money for talking about Gemma's suffering, so I asked some of the other parents on the ward what they thought. Most of them thought it was all right.

Steven sat and talked to the *News of the World* reporter in a hotel near the hospital, while I listened in. I was surprised by many of the things he said, not having appreciated how he must have felt. He confessed that he now backed my legal fight, although that put him in a difficult position as he was still employed at Sellafield. His work was still his livelihood and the only way in which he was able to support his family. He said how much he admired me for speaking out on the media, something he had never felt capable of doing. He was full of bitterness and cynicism towards the nuclear industry. The *News of the World* ran the story the following Sunday and paid us the money as promised. Most of it went in paying off our debts, although there was enough left over to buy some expensive presents, a trendy tracksuit for Richenda and an educational computer for Gemma. The money helped take our minds off things for a few days.

Although much of BNFL's reaction to the Gardner study was predictably defensive, a comment made a week later by the company's most senior health official kept the issue on the front pages. At a press conference after a meeting between Professor Gardner and BNFL's workforce at Sellafield, Dr Roger Berry, the company's health and safety director, was asked what advice he would give male workers who remained concerned about the risks of working at the plant. 'If someone is that worried, it may be the proper advice not to have a family,' he replied. 'Workers who want individual counselling can get it, and if they are so worried the advice could be: "Don't have children." It is not something, however, that I hope would be widespread advice.' Although BNFL later issued a statement insisting that it was not company policy to advise employees against becoming parents, the following day's headlines understandably highlighted Berry's remarks. 'If you don't want your children to be born with leukaemia,' screamed the *Daily Star*, 'DON'T HAVE KIDS!'

Throughout the length of my fight, no one from the nuclear industry ever officially made any direct contact with me or other members of my immediate family. But I did have one memorably weird unofficial approach, which convinced me never to allow into the house anyone I did not know or was not expecting. Late one afternoon, shortly after a renewed bout of publicity about Gemma, a thin, sallow, middle-aged man wearing a suit and tie that seemed far too big for him knocked on the door. Under his arm he was carrying a neatly folded newspaper with a picture of Gemma and me on the front. He introduced himself, saying he was from Sellafield and flashing a security pass similar to Steven's. I assumed at first that he might have come from BNFL to have a private word about the impending court case, although we later found out that he worked for a security company on the site. I showed him into the living room where Gemma was playing and offered him a cup of tea or coffee, which he declined.

He sat down and started telling me that he knew what caused leukaemia. 'It is Satan,' he said, staring at me. 'Satan is in your house. I can feel his presence. He is also in your daughter. I would like to perform an exorcism on her to rid her of Satan and cure her of leukaemia.' Although he was obviously crazy, what he said really scared me and I refused to let him do what he wanted. I kept looking hopefully out of the window, knowing that Steven was due back from work any minute. I tried to get him to leave, but he would not budge. Gemma started to giggle at him.

When Steven eventually appeared, I had no chance to warn him before the man stood up, shook his hand and repeated his unearthly theory about the origins of chronic myeloid leukaemia. 'I am a born-again Christian and I have read in the Bible of what Satan can do. I know he can take on many forms, and I sense his evil here in this house. I must perform an exorcism or at least a prayer to rid you of him.' Steven told him firmly that we were not religious, but for diplomacy's sake allowed him one prayer before showing him personally to the door. The man held Gemma's hands and started babbling about the devil and calling upon him to leave. The whole performance was too much for Gemma, who burst out laughing in his face. 'That is not Gemma laughing,' he ranted, 'it is Satan!'

Chapter 8

I Should Be So Lucky

'Mam, am I going to die?' Gemma looked questioningly up at me as we walked across the school playground hand in hand. She asked quite casually, as if she was asking what was for lunch, although it was clearly something she had been thinking about. I was taken by surprise and could not think what to say at first. Then I remembered a nurse at the hospital advising me never to lie. I took a deep breath.

'Yes, Gemma,' I said. I paused as Gemma explained how that morning one of her friends had told her that she was going to die. 'Mummy's going to die. Daddy's going to die. Richenda's going to die. All your friends are going to die. Everybody in the world dies some time. Just maybe you will die a little sooner,' I explained. 'That's why we need to find you a bone marrow transplant, so that you will die when you're older like most people.'

My explanation surprised me and seemed to be acceptable to Gemma. As we walked home she started asking me about heaven. I told her I had no real idea of what it was like, but suggested that she imagine it as anything she wanted it to be. Her vision was a huge fairground where everything was free – giant hot dogs, beefburgers and toffee apples. She had her own house on a pink cloud, with pink carpets and a pink three-piece suite. She asked if Janine, her dead baby sister, would be there. I said she would.

'When I die I'll take a baby bottle for Janine because she didn't have time to get one when she was here,' Gemma explained, staring up at the sky. 'I'll look after her until you and Daddy and Richenda get there. And I'll wait there for you.'

Gemma never seemed frightened of death. In a funny way I think she used to look forward to it, as if it was a special holiday. When people asked her how she was, she would give them a straightforward answer: 'I'm fine, but did you know I'm going to die?' This was partly because she liked to shock, but also because it just seemed like a relevant piece of factual information. Death is the only certainty in life, yet people hardly ever talk about it. Richenda hated Gemma talking about it as it upset her. But actually Gemma's matter-of-fact attitude made things easier for Steven and me. We could talk more openly in front of her, and somehow the stark, childlike simplicity of her understanding helped us come to terms with the reality of what was happening. It is only adults who fear death, because they know what they are leaving behind. Children regard it as another adventure.

In the autumn of 1989 Gemma started going to school a couple of mornings a week. The headmistress of the local infants' school, having heard about how the nursery had first refused and then offered a place, came to see us to suggest the arrangement. I think she understood my decision to reject the nursery, and was anxious to assure me that her school would take proper care of my daughter. She promised to contact me immediately she discovered that any children had contracted chicken pox or measles. She told me that her staff understood well how to look after children with leukaemia as they had recently had to deal with two other cases. I was impressed by her attitude and agreed that Gemma should attend.

Gemma was thrilled. The truth was that, since her cousin and best friend Bianca had started school, she was spending more time than she liked on her own. She especially liked the idea of wearing a school uniform, even though it was not compulsory. After the headmistress left, Gemma dragged me out to the shops where I bought her a crisp slate-grey pinafore, a gleaming white shirt and a bottle-green cardigan. Then we toured every shoe shop in Whitehaven until we found the perfect pair of black patent leather shoes, which she became very fond of. After school, she always used to clean them so they would be nice and shiny for the next day. She was very proud of her uniform and always tried to look her best in it.

Going to school for those few months became a routine that Gemma loved. We set off in the morning at 8.45, walking up to the fruit shop. We had to stop there because Gemma always bought a banana and an apple, while Richenda got a banana and an orange. They weren't allowed to take sweets to school. Richenda left us at the shop to walk to her junior school, which was about a quarter of a mile down the road, and Gemma came with me. When we arrived at her school, I took off her coat so she could hang it on her peg, which was identified by a bright blue boat. Then Gemma would take off, running towards the classroom. Realising that I was still there, she would turn back and shout, 'See ya, Mam.'

Meanwhile, I was becoming very pessimistic about our search for a bone marrow donor, which had now been in progress for more than two years with no tangible results. Then in September 1989 came a telephone call from Dr Jenny Kernahan in Newcastle, asking us to come to a meeting to discuss a new idea for treating Gemma. There we learned about a scheme called Bone Marrow 2000, which was based on the very latest medical technology. One of its advantages was that transplants could be tried using bone marrow which was not an absolutely perfect match. Steven's bone marrow, it turned out, had been very similar to Gemma's, although not similar enough for a conventional transplant. But with Bone Marrow 2000, doctors thought that it might be worth considering a transplant from him. They made it clear, though, that this was a very risky option that should only be considered in the absence of other suitable donors. There was still the danger that Gemma's body would recognise Steven's bone marrow as alien and reject it. The odds of success were put at about sixty to forty against. We were advised not to make an immediate decision, but to go away and think carefully about it.

We were dumbfounded, After all our searching, all our worrying and all our hoping, the key to Gemma's future could be no further away than her father. The first thought that flew through my head was that a 40 per cent chance of survival was much better than none – the odds that Gemma was currently facing. But the decision was not as simple as that. If the transplant failed it would leave her bone marrow so wrecked that it could not function for long. Instead of the possibility of surviving with the aid of chemotherapy for years, she could be facing death in weeks. We were being asked to gamble with the life of our daughter.

Postponing our decision, we felt that Steven should have further tests to ensure that his bone marrow was suitable. The results confirmed that the transplant could definitely go ahead and we learned more about what it would involve, some of which was very scary. In order to prepare Gemma's bone marrow to accept Steven's, her little body would have to be bombarded by large quantities of toxic drugs (chemotherapy) or high doses of radiation (radiotherapy), the purpose of which would be to destroy her bone marrow cells so that they would not reject the donated tissue. Unfortunately the treatment would also destroy other cells in the body, causing many short- and long-term side-effects. Gemma's hair was likely to fall out, she might feel nauseous, and she would probably suffer skin rashes, mouth ulcers, tummy aches and diarrhoea. Her liver could be damaged, she could develop eye cataracts and there was a possibility that she could be infertile in later life.

The treatment would also effectively suppress the body's natural defences against disease, rendering it very vulnerable to infection. This meant that Gemma would have to be strictly confined to a sterile environment for the duration of the treatment, which we were initially told would last between six and eight weeks. She would have to stay behind a sophisticated laminar air ventilation system, comprising a canopy over her bed that would blow a constant, flowing curtain of air all around her. She would not be allowed to step out through the invisible curtain, and no one would be allowed to step in without washing and putting on a gown, hat and mask. Doctors advised us that the need to take a decision was not urgent, but warned that treatment would be best carried out while Gemma was relatively healthy. In that sense, time was running out.

I asked Dr Kernahan what her professional advice would be. What decision should we take? Sensibly, I suppose, she ducked the question, saying that once we had been presented with the potential risks and benefits, it had to be entirely up to Steven and me. We asked Tina, my father and others close to us what they would do, but none of them could really say. We were yearning for someone else to take the decision away from us, someone other than ourselves to blame if it all went wrong. But I think deep down we knew that this was a choice that no one could make for us. It was the worst decision of our lives. Gemma's life was literally in our hands. If we said yes, she would experience pain, sickness and isolation – but with a 40 per cent chance of a reasonably good life afterwards. If we said no, Gemma could live for a few years longer – perhaps, if we were very lucky, for as long as ten years – but then she would die. It was hard, very hard.

It was made even harder by the fact that Steven and I disagreed. His first instinct was to say no, and give Gemma a few good years of life. Mine was to say yes, and give her at least the chance of a decent life. Every evening for three weeks we argued it through, trying to air all our fears and hopes. Sometimes we discussed it calmly and rationally, sometimes we let our fraught emotions get the better of us. I argued that because Gemma was just a child, she had no fear of death. But if she survived until she was fourteen, fifteen or sixteen, she might have close friends, perhaps even a boyfriend, and would start being afraid. She would begin to understand what she would leave behind in a way which a child of six could not. Gemma was also young enough, should the treatment be successful, to forget what an ordeal it was. Steven did not want to see her suffer pain now when her chances of living a good life as a result were so slender. Neither of course did I, but I felt strongly that we had to try. I could not have watched Gemma die in the knowledge that we had not tried.

Two days before we were due to return to Newcastle with our decision, Steven began to come round to my point of view. But before we finally decided to give the transplant the go-ahead, we asked Gemma what she thought. We were all sitting round the kitchen table having tea when Steven announced that he had some good news. Gemma and Richenda stopped eating and looked up. We explained what the hospital had said as best we could, and asked Gemma what she would like to do. Her answer ensured that our decision was at last made. She said, as she had always said, that she wanted to catch chicken pox and measles. But she added with a cheeky grin: 'If it's Dad's bone marrow, I'll probably get drunk.'

It seemed so right to me that Steven and Gemma should share the same tissue because they were so alike in their character – like two peas in a pod, everyone used to say. There was also a bizarre symmetry in the idea that the man whose sperm, if Professor Gardner's hypothesis was accurate, could have given Gemma her illness was now the man whose bone marrow might cure her. We explained to Richenda that Gemma, Steven and I would be away for at least six weeks and that she would have to stay with Tina and Russell. We said she would be able to visit at weekends and that we would come home whenever we could. 'Don't worry,' we tried to reassure her, 'six weeks seems like a long time now, but it will pass pretty quickly.'

When we told Dr Kernahan that we wanted to go ahead with the transplant, she suggested that treatment could start almost immediately, in November. I desisted, however, because I wanted all the family to enjoy Gemma's sixth birthday and Christmas together first. Dr Kernahan agreed, and we settled on Tuesday, 9 January 1990 as her admission date.

I wanted Gemma's birthday to be her most memorable yet. For once Helen and I agreed not to celebrate her daughter Kerry's birthday at the same time, so that the focus would be entirely on Gemma. We enquired about getting someone professional to make a special birthday cake, and a local woman insisted on donating one when she heard who it was for. The cake she made was quite extraordinary: it was shaped like a princess's castle, and all the multi-coloured decoration was edible. Gemma invited all her new friends from school as well as her old friends from home. We hired the local church hall, carried over a stereo and bought her a new bike, as she had outgrown the one she had been given two years earlier.

Gemma sat with her cousin Bianca and her new friend Caroline at the centre of a U-shaped arrangement of tables laden with sandwiches and fairy cakes. After eating, we played pass-the-parcel and musical statues before we got all the children to shout for the day's surprise visitor: Tina's husband Russell, dressed up as Santa Claus on an early pre-Christmas visit. To everyone's delight he rode in on Gemma's new bike, ho-ho-hoing for all he was worth. After distributing presents he had to retire quickly when his son, Nikki, asked why he was wearing his Dad's watch. Gemma was deeply thrilled by the whole occasion and told us so afterwards.

She enjoyed her Christmas, too. We have a videotape of her and Bianca dancing wildly around the living room on Christmas Day to a hit song by Kylie Minogue, who later sent Gemma a letter in hospital. 'Lucky, lucky, lucky, I should be so lucky,' they sing, as they tear breathlessly around the room with hair and dresses flying.

To see in the New Year, we all went round to Tina's. I have a very clear memory of Steven sitting in Tina's reclining chair with Gemma, who was finding it very hard to stay awake. At the stroke of midnight, the room was filled with silence. When I looked over at Steven, he had his head on Gemma's head and tears were streaming down his face. 'I love you, Gem,' he whispered.

'I love you too, Dad,' responded Gemma. 'Happy New Year.'

'I hope it is, Gem, I hope it is.'

Gemma was admitted to Ward 16 South in Newcastle's Royal Victoria Infirmary on 9 January as planned. It had been two and a half years since we entered the ward on that fateful day when her leukaemia had first been diagnosed. It looked just as depressing as it did then, with some beds empty and some occupied by children, many of whom had lost their hair and were in obvious discomfort. Gemma, carrying her own little bag containing her pyjamas, her slippers and a couple of toys she had been given for Christmas, was shown to her bed by a nurse. I think she was a little scared.

Her first stay in hospital was only for two days. The purpose was to fit what is known as a Hickman line, or more colloquially, a 'long line'. This was a narrow plastic tube that was surgically inserted into a major blood vessel in the chest through a hole in the skin on the stomach. It meant that blood samples could be taken and large amounts of drugs administered without the need for skin-puncturing injections. The line could also be used, as we later discovered, for performing the bone marrow transplant itself.

Just before Gemma was due to go into surgery, a nurse asked if she would like to see one of the other children's long lines, so that she knew what it would be like. We all went over to the bed of a boy called Josh, who happily lifted his pyjama top to reveal a long, thin, soft tube sealed with a screw cap emerging from a tiny slit in his stomach, all neatly held in place by a special piece of white sticky tape. Josh peeled back the tape so that we could get a better look. Gemma screwed up her face as if it looked painful. 'It doesn't hurt,' said Josh, looking at her. The nurse told me that I would have to learn how to use and clean the line, a very complex procedure using a special sterility pack to reduce the risk of infection.

Steven and I accompanied Gemma to the operating theatre, where she was given the usual 'magic wind'. After about an hour's wait, she was brought back to her bed. Her stomach was orange because it had been smeared with a powerful sterile liquid. Like Josh, she had a piece of white sticky tape over a thin plastic tube, but unlike him, her tube ended with two sealed caps instead of one: her treatment was to be more intensive than his. While Gemma was sleeping, a nurse showed me how to use the sterility pack. I had to wash my hands in a sterile solution, wash a metal trolley with sterile wipes and then peel open the pack. On top was a yellow plastic bag, which was fixed to the trolley as a waste container. Then I had to open another sealed white parcel without letting my bare hands touch the inside, and put on a pair of sterile gloves. That done, I had to prepare a plastic tray by pouring sterile liquid into it and laying out cotton wool. There were two pairs of plastic tweezers, which could only be used once for holding the line before they had to be discarded. Using a dummy long line, I had to learn how to take off the cap and squirt in liquid with a syringe. I had to practise this process many times before I could trust myself to perform it on Gemma.

When Gemma came round she was wary of the sticky tape on her tummy, and anxious to prevent anyone from touching it in case it hurt. A nurse eventually persuaded her to allow it to be peeled back. The tiny slit in her stomach looked sore, like a fresh wound. When unravelled, the tube was surprisingly long, its two caps dangling at the top of Gemma's knee when she stood up. When she had overcome the strangeness, she became quite proud of her long line, even awarding it a special name, 'Wigglies'. She liked nothing more than to stand and swirl her stomach so that the line swung around fast like a fan, a game that we had to put a stop to for fear of her injuring someone.

We were allowed home for a week before the transplant itself began. Gemma proudly showed all her friends and relatives her Wigglies, just to emphasise how special she was. She had to go into the local hospital to have two teeth removed so that there was no chance that they would cause her trouble during her treatment. The staff at the hospital were all fascinated by her Wigglies, as most of them had only read about such devices in medical textbooks. I insisted that the line should be used to administer the anaesthetic so that Gemma did not have to suffer a needle, but this created problems as there was only a handful of doctors in the hospital who knew how to use it. When her teeth had been removed, Gemma kept them in a jar beside her bed. I think she imagined that if she ran out of money, she could slip them under her pillow to get some more from the tooth fairy.

We decided she should have her hair cut, too, so that when it fell out it would not be so traumatic and messy. The first stage was to cut it back to shoulder length, which made Gemma look very mature and attractive. In hospital we had it cut much shorter. The evening before we were due to return to Newcastle, Tina took Gemma and Bianca out to bingo in the church hall, where the prizes were always food. Gemma had never won before, but that evening she was lucky, winning some steak, onions and peas. She gave them to my father for him to keep until she came home. He laughed and said he would.

The following morning we took Richenda round to Tina's, said goodbye and set off for a whole new way of life. When I first saw Gemma's treatment room, with her bed under the specially rigged-up sterile ventilation system, I was relieved at the amount of space she appeared to have. But then I watched as staff carefully unrolled some large sticky red tape on the floor all around the bed, no more than two feet away. When the air machine was turned on, no one was allowed to step inside the red line without washing and gowning up. A nurse explained to Gemma that she was not allowed under any circumstances to step outside the line, because if she did she might catch an infection and die.

The room itself, in which Gemma had to spend far longer than we initially imagined, was quite small. It had a sink in one corner, and near the window a coat-stand on which several clean white gowns always hung. On the window ledge were two boxes, one with paper hats designed to cover your hair and the other with paper masks that covered your mouth and nose. They could only be used once and then had to be thrown away. Out of the window you could see a flat roof and part of a dirty old college building, but no trees or grass. You could not see the road unless you stood right next to the window, but you could hear the traffic day and night. Whenever goals were scored at the nearby St James's Park football ground, you could hear the roars.

The doctors decided that, instead of subjecting Gemma to total body irradiation to kill off her bone marrow in preparation for the transplant, they would first try chemotherapy. They started with a high dose of busulphan, which had previously been very effective in causing her bone marrow to collapse. Her daily dose consisted of at least twenty tablets, which she preferred to liquid medicine because they had no taste. To the amazement of nurses, she liked swallowing them one at a time. Later, drugs were administered as a liquid through the long line. After four days on busulphan, it was time to turn on the air flow and confine Gemma to her red-line prison.

It was hard to get used to the new routine. Several times, without thinking, I nearly stepped over the red line without gowning up – which always seemed to take ages. When I was within the red line with Gemma I could cuddle her and tickle her, but because of the mask I could never give her a kiss, which upset me. The challenge in such difficult circumstances was to keep her stimulated and amused, prevent her from going crazy and help her distinguish between day and night. We decided always to try and change her into her day clothes in the morning and her pyjamas in the evening, although that did not always work. Another problem was the food, which had to be tinned or frozen to reduce the risk of contamination. The hospital dietician, told that Gemma liked sausages and meatballs, provided tins of nothing but. Steven and I, who were staying in a parents' room at the other end of the hospital, ended up trying to shop for Gemma's food ourselves to try and create some diversity.

At the same time Steven had to have his bone marrow removed. He was admitted to Ward 13 and taken to the operating theatre in the afternoon. His mother and Tina had come across to help me as I shuttled between him and Gemma. I was worried about him, because I knew how he hated hospitals and needles. It was strange and sad, too, because this was the first time we had really been parted since Gemma had been diagnosed. After the operation, which lasted about an hour, Tina and I went to see him in the recovery room. He was groggy and kept drifting in and out of sleep. He was wearing a small green oxygen mask and had heart monitors all over his chest, which the nurse assured us was routine. On his hand there was a black crocodile clip which shone an infra-red light through the top of his finger. He held this finger at an odd angle pointing into the air, which made Tina smile. He said he was fine.

By about seven o'clock that evening Steven had recovered sufficiently to want to go and see Gemma, despite the fact that he was on a drip in his hand to replenish some of the fluid he had lost. The nurse insisted that he went in a wheelchair, but then could only find one with flat tyres. We made slow progress along the corridors, with Steven's free hand holding and pushing his drip-stand and me struggling with the disabled wheelchair. When Gemma asked if he was all right, Steven said he was a little sore. Her response was not very sympathetic: 'Now you know how I felt when I had it done.' Steven actually looked deathly pale, and was not looking forward to having to spend a night on the ward. After a while Gemma seemed to become disturbed by the sight of her Dad sitting in a wheelchair looking so ill, so I suggested that he return to his bed.

There he begged me to find a way for him to have a cigarette.

Although it really was not allowed, the ward sister said it would be all right and directed us to the television room at the end of the ward. It was full of chairs lined up with their backs against the wall, the most uncomfortable of which Steven decided to sit on. I handed him a cigarette and warned him to take it easy. He took one drag and put it down in the ashtray beside him. 'I feel really funny,' he said. 'I feel like I'm going to faint.' I suggested that he put his head between his legs and went to help him by putting my arms under his. Suddenly his head just flopped like a dead weight. I lifted it and saw his face. It looked ghastly, without any trace of colour. His eyes were still open and his mouth looked crooked.

In panic I yelled for help and the ward sister rushed in, quickly followed by a nurse. They laid Steven on the floor, tapped his face and gave him a heart massage. I started screaming because I thought he was dead. A visitor who happened to be in the room held me tight, assuring me that he was all right and would come round soon. When he did, he looked bewildered and sorrowful. The nurse asked if I would like to give him a hug. I said that I would prefer to kick him for giving me such a fright. I really thought for a moment that he had gone. I know it is a cliché, but I did not realise how much I loved him until I nearly lost him.

I was still in shock later when I burst into tears telling Tina what had happened. She gave me a vodka to calm me down, which worked as I do not usually drink. I heard her talking to Russell on the telephone about the children baking cakes at home and thought that the conversation sounded a little odd. Tina stayed with Gemma that night, so that I was able to get a good sleep in the parents' room. It was not until the next morning that Tina told me that Richenda had been in hospital overnight after suffering concussion caused by a fall at school, but that she was better now. Tina had hidden the incident from me so that I did not have any more to worry about. They say that unhappy events come in threesomes. In the space of twenty-four hours, the three people I loved most in the world – Steven, Richenda and Gemma – had all been sick in hospital for different reasons. My nerves were so jangled up that all I could do was laugh.

The act of giving Gemma Steven's bone marrow was very simple. A doctor holding a large syringe full of a yellowish substance pumped it into Gemma's body via her long line. It took no more than twenty minutes. When the operation was completed, Gemma waved her head around and pretended to be drunk on her father's alcoholic tissue. Then began the waiting game, when the challenge was to keep her amused. We were told that it would take at least ten to fourteen days before we could hope to see any improvement in her bone marrow function. The key was her blood count. The chemotherapy had reduced her white blood count to around 0.1. If the transplant was going to be successful, we needed to see that number rise by at least ten times. The daily notification of Gemma's white blood count began to dominate our lives. To keep a record of it, Steven and I began writing every day in a Greenpeace diary that someone had given us. The date was Thursday, 25 January 1990: Day 1.

Although we were anxious to see Richenda after her accident, we did not want Gemma to realise that we were not with her as she seemed to gain a great deal of comfort and reassurance from our constant presence. So after she had fallen asleep in the evening, we drove the hundred miles home. It was late when we arrived, and the first thing I did was to ring the hospital to make sure Gemma was still asleep. Richenda was very glad to see us and proudly showed us the bump on her head, which she insisted was no longer sore. We set off back to the hospital early the next morning and arrived on the ward a few minutes after Gemma had woken up. She was a little concerned about where we had been. 'Just for a coffee,' said Steven.

On Day 7 – the seventh day after the transplant – Gemma's hair started to fall out. It suddenly seemed to be everywhere – all over her pillow, her sheets, her cover and the floor, not dropping out in thick lumps but thinning fast. One evening she sat and tugged at it, until she had managed to remove sizeable chunks. She thought it was funny, although it looked painful. The more we told her to stop, the more she delighted in plucking herself like a chicken. When she eventually stopped, she had created her first bald patch.

Against my wishes, she insisted on having a mirror to see what it looked like. Warning her that she would be shocked and upset, I washed, gowned up and sterilised her little pink mirror. Inevitably, she cried when she saw what she had done. She thought it looked horrible. I tried to comfort her by telling her that it would all grow back when her treatment was over. Before then, I said, the hospital would provide a wig of whatever colour and length she chose.

The next day I arranged for Gemma's head to be measured for an NHS wig. She chose hair slightly darker than her own, and longer so that it could be plaited. She did not seem dismayed that the wig would take ten days to make, partly because she had begun to feel distinctly unwell. The chemotherapy was making her feel nauseous, her temperature topped 40° centigrade (140° Fahrenheit), and she was sleeping much of the time. With her face and cheeks all puffed up from the drugs, she had started for the first time to look as if she was really ill. Disappointingly, though it was now Day 10, her white blood count was still hovering around 0.1. But we were assured it was still early days.

When she was well enough, Gemma would help a nurse strip and make her bed in the morning, before she got changed into her day clothes. Always staying within the red line, she walked around the bed, following the nurse's instructions. She soon became proficient at folding the blankets in traditional 'hospital corners'. Because Gemma was unable to play with the ordinary, unsterilised toys on the ward, the hospital offered to pay for some new ones specially for her. But it was not until I got to the shop with a member of staff that I was told that £20 was the limit. I added another £50, although we could not really afford it, so we could get her some good puzzles and games. Because Steven had stopped working, cash was becoming very tight, a situation only relieved by regular donations from both our fathers.

The first time Tina, Russell, Richenda and Bianca came to visit, Gemma was worried about being seen without any hair – so we bought her a baseball cap. She insisted on keeping the door and the blind on the door closed until she was ready to receive her visitors, her new cap drawn firmly over her head. When she told me to pull up the blind and they all peered in, she looked straight at them and, with a huge grin, lifted her cap straight off. Richenda did not seem too bothered, but Tina, Russell and Bianca were shocked at how different she looked. It does not matter how much you verbally prepare people for the sight of serious illness, it always takes them by surprise. 'Hello, baldy,' said Tina. 'Russell can polish that for you when he's cleaning up.'

Gemma told Bianca that when her hair grew back it would be darker than hers and would reach past her bottom. This seemed to put Bianca more at ease, since she recognised the cheek as Gemma's. 'She may look different on the outside, but she's the same on the inside,' we told her. Gemma had other visitors that day and, though she adored being the centre of so much attention, she ended up very tired, complaining of a tummy ache. She was also jealous because Richenda was staying with Steven and me in the parents' room. She wanted to be with us too, and it did not matter how many times I explained how impossible that was. She went to sleep unhappy.

Since Gemma had first joked about the notion of getting drunk on Steven's bone marrow, she had decided that she should drink like her Dad, who liked a lager or two in the evening. When we asked the doctor for advice he said that a strong black stout would not do any harm as long as it did not get out of control, and it might even do her some good. So we let Gemma try a can of Mackeson, which she liked. Then we started giving her a small, ice-cold can every now and again as a treat if she had been good. She quickly grew fond of her 'Mackie', as she called it. It was funny in the evening to watch Steven sitting in the chair just outside the red line sipping his lager and Gemma sitting up in bed with her Mackie. She always slept well those nights.

On Day 13, one of the doctors came and excitedly told us what her blood count was. For the first time it was 0.2, where it remained uncertainly for a few days. This did represent an improvement, though only a very slight one. We needed a reading of at least double that before we could allow ourselves any optimism. Gemma was still feeling intermittently sick and complaining of aching limbs. Because her lips were swollen, she bit the skin off and made them bleed. On one occasion she reacted badly to a transfusion of platelets, the cells in the blood that help prevent and control bleeding. I returned from showing someone out to find Gemma sitting on the bed shaking from head to toe. Surrounded by anxious-looking nurses, she was laughing at the water that was jumping violently out of the cup she was holding. It took a full ten minutes for her to calm down after a nurse had given her some drugs. Then she felt suddenly tired and fell asleep.

Steven started going home during the week so that he could work at Sellafield again in order to bring in some money. The first evening he was not there I wrote in the diary, 'Missing Steven terribly.' Gemma, used to his constant presence, became quite upset and started to miss him too, and we were both very glad when he came for visits. I grew quite anxious about Gemma's isolation and tried to think of ways of keeping her in touch. I thought it might help if Gemma had access to a portable telephone, which could be sterilised. I went into the British Telecom shop in Newcastle, explained Gemma's problem and enquired about hiring a phone for two weeks. The woman behind the desk said nothing, got up and fetched a mobile phone from a drawer. She put it with a battery charger into a BT bag and gave it to me. It was only on my way out of the shop that I realised that I had not left my name and address. I went back to give them and the woman just smiled and nodded. I do not know to this day whether she realised how much joy her simple act gave Gemma.

Steven and I made her a huge poster listing all the names and telephone numbers of her friends and relatives, each one in a different colour so that she did not get them mixed up. The first person she rang was Tina, who was working in her shop. When the customers heard who it was they all shouted 'Get well soon' and told Tina not to hurry. Gemma quickly learned how to telephone Steven's father at work in Sellafield. It was not long before British Nuclear Fuels' switchboard operators recognised her voice and, after asking how she was, put her straight through to her Grandad. She took to keeping the phone constantly by her side and creating mischief by ringing up nurses' boyfriends to ask them whether they were in love. The phone also became invaluable to Steven and me. On the very few occasions when we both left the hospital, we managed to persuade Gemma to allow us to take it so that we could be contacted wherever we were.

By Day 19 Gemma's white blood count had sunk back to 0.1, and it soon became clear that the transplant had failed. The doctors were reassuring, saying that it often did not work first time. Since Gemma still seemed quite strong they suggested a second attempt after a two-week rest, this time using some different drugs. We agreed – not that by then we had any real choice. Because of the chemotherapy there was virtually nothing left of Gemma's bone marrow. She could not survive on her own for long outside her sterile curtain of air.

As the weeks became months on the leukaemia ward, we made many good friends amongst the other parents. We used to support each other, babysit for each other and even share the odd Chinese take-away in the parents' rooms. We would talk about our children, our common experiences, our doubts and deepest fears. We shared an impatience with outsiders, those normal people with everyday worries who appeared on visits and then disappeared again. We found it hard to tolerate their mindless talk of matching curtains and carpets, of the prices of things in shops, of the problems of public transport. To us such things seemed so irrelevant, so inconsequential.

In the next room to Gemma was a little girl called Lesley, who was suffering from something similar to leukaemia. She had a different kind of transplant, called an autograft, which involved removing some of her relatively unaffected bone marrow at an early stage and then returning it later on in the hope that it would aid recovery. Lesley reacted to her own bone marrow by turning as red as a tomato, which looked alarming but did not seem to do her any great damage. Lesley's mother, Cindy, was a large, cheerful woman with a strong Geordie accent. We often used to go for coffee and a cigarette together.

A small boy called David, who had another kind of cancer, also had an autograft. He was fine for the first two weeks afterwards, but then his kidneys started to fail. He was moved to intensive care, where he eventually died. Steven and I went to his funeral, the first we had ever been to for a child. David's parents, Margaret and Keith, were a tower of strength and gave us great support. Even after David died, they kept returning to the ward to see everyone. David's death prompted a lot of questions from Gemma. Why hadn't his cancer gone away? Where did his body go? Was he in heaven? We tried to answer them as straightforwardly as we could, but it was not easy.

Then there was the tragic case of Amy, the eighteen-month-old daughter of Denise and Steven. She had leukaemia and had failed to respond to any treatment. After doctors said there was no more they could do, Denise and Steven decided to take Amy home. Before she left, I asked Denise what would happen without any antibiotics or treatment. As soon as the words were out of my mouth, I realised what a stupid question it was. Denise did not answer and walked away with tears rolling down her face. I was sure that Denise would change her mind, but she never did. She brought Amy to say goodbye to Gemma and we all cried.

After she had gone I talked to Alison, another good friend whose twelve-year-old son was being treated for a tumour. We decided that Denise's decision was very humane and very courageous, although we doubted whether we could have made it. We could not stop thinking about her, so we bought some flowers and a bottle of wine and caught a taxi to her house. When she answered the door, she said we were welcome to come in but Amy might die at any moment. I was scared. I had never seen anyone die before, let alone a baby. When we walked in Steven, Amy's father, was sitting in a chair cradling her in his arms. Her breathing was very laboured and loud. Alison and I went over and talked to her as if she could understand us. We sat around and talked about the hospital until suddenly Amy fell silent. I had imagined that we would all dissolve into tears, but she looked so calm, so free of the pain that had afflicted her short life, that sorrow seemed superfluous. As Denise held her saying her final farewells, Amy seemed to be smiling, at peace at last. It was one of the most beautiful sights I have ever seen.

Once again Gemma was full of unanswerable questions. Did

Amy cry? Where had she gone? Was she in the free fairground in heaven? Did she have her own pink cloud and furniture? She coped by deciding that Janine would now have someone to play with. She asked me specially to tell Denise and Steven not to cry, because she was sure that Amy was happy.

Gemma was now starting to get very fed up with her prison. I desperately wanted to allow her some more freedom, perhaps even a walk around the room. The staff explicitly forbade it, but came up with some alternative suggestions. One was to replace Gemma's bed temporarily with a chair, which would give her more sense of space. Steven and I gowned up, stepped over the red line and pushed out her bed as she stood watching. A nurse, having thoroughly cleaned a chair with sterile wipes, handed it in to us. It was lovely to see Gemma walking around and sitting in the chair, but after a while she became tired and asked for her bed back. This meant stripping it, sterilising it and pushing it back. Gemma slept well that night, and asked us to repeat the performance every two hours the following day. 'God, I'm knackered,' Steven wrote in the diary.

In the two weeks between the failure of the first transplant and the start of the second, I went home for a weekend to celebrate my birthday. Gemma telephoned me at least twenty times a day to ask what I was doing and when I would be back to see her. She loved giving presents and had already got Tina, who had volunteered to stay with her in hospital, to run a series of shopping errands at her expense for my birthday. At five o'clock in the morning on the day I was due back, Gemma rang Tina in the parents' room and demanded to see her. Tina, thinking it might be serious, got up and rushed along the corridor to see what was the matter. Gemma, sitting up in bed, asked if she could light the candles on my birthday cake as she wanted to be sure to surprise me. Tina, understandably angry, threatened to kill her and explained that I was not due to arrive until dinner time. Oblivious, Gemma asked if they could wrap my presents instead. Her anger quickly fading, Tina agreed. When I arrived, Gemma ordered Tina to hand me the presents. The biggest surprise was a cake laden with candles, which Gemma and I sat and ate while watching television.

Tina remembers another occasion when she and Russell promised to make Gemma a big fish tank out of paper and boxes, with the idea of involving her in lots of colouring. 'The first mistake I made was to tell her on Friday night that we'd get started early on Saturday morning when the shops opened,' Tina recalled.

> At six o'clock in the morning we had a telephone call in the parents' room asking us to go and see Gemma, which we did (rush rush rush). When we got there she wanted to know what time the shops opened. 'In three hours,' I told her, and she turned over to go back to sleep. Russell and I, however, were up and dressed with nothing to do. At half-past eight we went down to the shops and bought lots of colouring pens, coloured paper and sticky things. Gemma was keen to start as soon as we got back. After half an hour she demanded the television be put on and sat and watched it all day without touching another colouring pen. Meanwhile Russell and I wore ourselves out colouring, cutting, sticking. All Gemma kept saying was: 'Not finished yet!'

The second night after Gemma restarted chemotherapy, she vomited four times. The anti-sickness drugs that the nurses gave her made her sleep most of the next day. She started having regular nose bleeds, which she hated, and her whole face began to puff up, making her almost unrecognisable. To prepare Steven for his second donation of bone marrow, doctors drew off some blood which was returned after the operation in order to try and prevent him from passing out again. As a result he was much better, perky even, when the second operation was completed. As his vital yellow jelly was squirted slowly into Gemma's long line, despite her nausea she said it felt like good stuff that would work this time. Only the awful waiting game and the daily blood counts would tell whether she was right. We were back to Day 1.

Apart from a swollen face and an unpleasant rash on her hands and feet, Gemma was reasonably fine until Day 6 of the second transplant when her blood pressure dropped and her temperature rose. The following day she started having difficulty breathing, which was really frightening. Tests revealed that she had at least two bugs in her blood, and doctors conducted a chest X-ray with a portable machine that they had sterilised as much as possible. They put her on antibiotics, which cured her after a few days. We knew she was getting better when she starting asking for her Mackie again. When she was well her taste for strong stout was becoming an obsession. We had started off allowing her a small can with the television at seven o'clock, when Steven had his lager. But she soon managed to talk Steven into allowing her to have one earlier, at six or even five o'clock.

Then, at one o'clock one morning she woke up and told the male nurse on duty that she was thirsty. But she refused water, demanding instead a can of Mackie from the fridge. When she threatened to scream, he said he would give it to her as long as she only had a sip. But of course as soon as Gemma had the can, she gulped down the lot before he could take it away. As a result she was heartily sick, and the poor nurse had to wake me in the parents' room. When I arrived on the scene, Gemma was sitting there smelling of vomit looking very pleased with herself while the nurse showered me with apologies. I tried to tell Gemma off, but I did not really have the heart. What the hell if she wants a can of Mackie at one in the morning? I thought. What other pleasures did she have?

On another occasion, when Tina and Russell were staying in the parents' room, Gemma made Russell come and see her at about four o'clock in the morning on the pretext of a sore back. She then asked him if he was thirsty and suggested they both have a drink. 'We sat together in the peace of the early morning, supping our cans of Mackie,' Russell recalled. Gemma thought that Russell was easily duped and once persuaded Tina to fill his can of Mackie with vinegar, which he pretended to drink while saying how funny it tasted. Gemma laughed until the tears rolled down her face.

I think she became addicted to her Mackie. She took to having one can with her lunch, another with her tea and a third before she went to sleep. It seemed to be the only drink that would quench her thirst. Somebody even brought her a special etched Mackeson glass. To make sure that she never ran out, she would ask visitors who walked past the door to bring her a four-pack. One evening, when Steven forgot to go to the off-licence, she was very upset. But then she telephoned the boyfriend of one of the mothers on the ward and asked him to get some on his way in. When at last he arrived, he pretended that he had forgotten, which made Gemma furious. It was only when he produced the required four-pack that peace broke out.

Towards the end of March, Steven worked out that it had been eighty days since Gemma had first been admitted. 'Could have been round the world,' he noted in the diary. Gemma had been trapped behind the red line for two months – sick, swollen and plagued with a skin rash – with no noticeable improvement in her condition. We had seen winter snow turn to spring rain out of her window, but no significant rise in her blood count, no change in her bone marrow. It was not surprising that she started getting depressed, and so did I.

On Day 10 of the second transplant she persuaded me to do something I should not have done. She begged me to allow her outside the red line. I closed the door to her room, pulled down the blind and put a mask on her. I reminded her that I was not supposed to let her out, but made her promise to keep it a secret. Very nervously she crossed the line, sat in the chair that I usually sat in, and then rushed back, frightened at what she had done. She could not have been outside her prison for more than thirty seconds. I felt very guilty and would have blamed myself if anything had happened as a result. Gemma never asked to go outside the line again.

Up to Day 15 Gemma's white blood count mostly failed to rise above 0.0. On Day 16 – April Fool's Day – it registered 0.3 for the first time and our hopes began to stir. On Day 17 we were told in the morning that it was 0.4, and I joked that I needed a Valium to calm my excitement. Gemma was very lively, and hungry too. But then later in the day a doctor told us that the figure had been checked and turned out to be an error. Gemma's real blood count was 0.1, around which it remained for the next few days. 'Very disheartened and angry,' reads Steven's diary entry. 'Don't believe the counts at all.'

Gemma cheered up a little when a new boy called Gary moved in opposite, especially when she learned that he too would have to be confined behind a curtain of air in preparation for a bone marrow transplant. His parents gave him a water gun, which he fired at the nurses. Gemma thought this was hilarious, and talked the same male nurse who had given her a Mackie into giving her a 50-millilitre plastic syringe. She then asked for a bowl of water on the pretext that she wanted to bath her doll. Requesting the nurse to come as close as possible, she squirted him full in the face. Then, along with Gary, she sprayed anyone who walked past. The corridor ended up like a swimming pool, and the gun and the syringe were confiscated.

After Day 23, with Gemma's count at 0.0, the doctors suggested that we met them to review her faltering treatment plan. They thought that one explanation as to why Steven's bone marrow had not taken was that the busulphan could have destroyed the scaffolding in Gemma's marrow, leaving Steven's nothing to graft on to. The only way to bring it back would be to keep Gemma behind the red line for months, which would obviously be very distressing for her. There was also the possibility of attempting a third transplant. After some discussion it was decided that, if there was no improvement in the next week, they would extract a bone marrow sample from Gemma to see what was going on. In the meantime a new drug would be tried to see if it helped.

Soon after that Gemma started to suffer serious pain in her legs and her mouth became very sore, as well as developing another infection. A problem with her liver made her constipated, swelled her stomach and turned her skin yellow. Sometimes she looked as if she was in agony. For the first time the doctors decided to give her a small dose of morphine, which worried me because I had seen other children on the ward become addicted to it. But it made her so much happier, even prompting her to ask for a Mackie. On Good Friday she was well enough to bake little Easter cakes with Tina and me. We took it in turns to sit behind the red line with her, mixing sterilised eggs and sterilised water. Each cake had either red, green or blue food colouring added to it and tiny chocolate eggs on top. When we had finished, Gemma and I sat on the bed offering the cakes to everyone that passed by.

On Easter Day I was woken at three o'clock in the morning by a nurse, who said Gemma wanted me. When I reached her room, she was sitting up in bed crying her eyes out. 'What's wrong?' I asked, trying to gown up as quickly as I could.

'I need a cuddle,' she said.

I stepped over the line and gave her the cuddle to end all cuddles. She calmed down, but carried on sobbing and I started to join in. The next thing I knew I was being woken up by a nurse. We were both lying on the bed, me all gowned up, still locked in an embrace. Gemma told me she was sorry for getting me out of my bed. I said I did not mind because I had needed a cuddle too, although perhaps I had not realised it.

With Gemma's white blood count remaining around 0.1, the doctors decided to go ahead with extracting a sample, or aspirate, of her bone marrow. This was an unpleasant operation at the best of times, but the conditions in which it had to be performed within the red line beggared belief. Gemma was anxious about it, so Steven and I promised her it would not hurt and that one of us would stay with her. Two doctors and a nurse wheeled in a metal trolley, gowned up and changed Gemma into an operating gown. They gave her a large dose of tranquilliser via her long line and laid out a gruesome-looking set of tools, including something that looked like a large corkscrew. Unfortunately, the tranquilliser did not seem to work properly. Although it made Gemma feel dizzy and disoriented, it did not put her to sleep. Horrifyingly, she seemed quite conscious of what was going on and started to cry. When the doctors pinned down her arms and legs and started to twist in the corkscrew, she screamed an unearthly scream.

Unable to bear it, I had long since left the room. Steven was asked to leave, and both of us were prevented from going back in by nurses at the door. We stared out of a window in the ward, holding each other tight, listening to Gemma's repeated screams:

'Help me, please help me. Mam, Dad.' There was nothing we could do to put her out of her misery. It was absolutely agonising. I shall never, as long as I live, forget her screams. After about half an hour the doctors came out, clearly shaken and very apologetic about what had happened. They did not understand why Gemma had been able to resist the tranquilliser, but said she would be all right if a little sore. They said we could go in and see her.

'You promised, you promised it wouldn't hurt. And you promised you wouldn't leave,' Gemma yelled at us with pure hatred in her eyes. After we succeeded in calming her down, she fell sound asleep for six hours. Amazingly, when she woke up the drug had completely erased any memory of what had happened. That made it easier for us to cope with, and took away some of the guilt. She had a huge appetite, and demanded a Mackie. Because of her new drugs regime that was now explicitly forbidden, so instead we gave her low alcohol lager which seemed to do.

The results of the bone marrow aspirate confirmed what we already knew: that the second transplant had failed. The doctors then seriously suggested attempting a third. This was highly unusual, as patients who have endured two transplants are rarely fit enough to face another one. Yet, despite everything, Gemma was still quite strong and seemed able to bounce back from her various relapses. Because the treatment was so expensive there had been some difficulty in persuading the hospital management that a third attempt was justified. But when we were offered it we had to go for it, hoping against hope that it would be third time lucky. If this one failed, as one of the doctors put it, we would have nothing left to do other than to take Gemma wherever she would be happiest.

The plan for the third transplant was to use the treatment that had been rejected in the first two: whole body radiotherapy. Instead of the toxic chemicals involved in chemotherapy, Gemma was to be deliberately exposed to radiation, similar to that which I blamed for causing her illness in the first place. Because this could not be carried out in the Royal Victoria Infirmary, we had to move to another hospital about five minutes away. Gemma, in other words, was going to escape from within the red line. To mark the occasion,

I bought her a whole new set of clothes – pants, socks, jeans, shirt, coat, trainers, the lot. She had to wear a mask, and insisted that her new cuddly toy bulldog, whom she had named Butch, had to wear one too. Refusing to get on the trolley that the ambulance men brought, she demanded a wheelchair instead.

She took a lot of convincing that it was all right to step over the red line, but once free she stared with wonder at everything she passed. She squinted at the daylight when we got outside, and shivered at the fresh air. When the ambulance drove past a park, she could hardly contain her excitement. 'Mam, look, there's a tree,' she shouted. 'It's got leaves on. Look, there's a dog. It's running.' The rest of us take such simple sights for granted, but for Gemma, who had seen nothing in recent memory but her room and rooftops, they were an unparalleled joy. When she went into hospital the trees had lost all their leaves; now they were blooming. When she asked the ambulance men to put on their 'der-ders', they happily turned on their siren.

We had grown used to the Royal Victoria Infirmary, its staff and its rules. It was hard to adapt to the new hospital, which seemed to be much stricter. Gemma was put under another sterile air flow, but not even allowed to leave her bed. Her room looked out through French windows on to an empty playground. She started feeling a little sick and developed a large blood blister on her tongue. I had to argue with the staff to persuade them to allow me to sleep on a camp bed in her room. To reach the radiotherapy machine, we had to wear masks and wheel Gemma through the hospital early in the morning or late at night when it was not too busy.

The first time she went for treatment, she was remarkably good. She had to lie still on her own in the middle of a darkened room surrounded by what looked like small sandbags while she was zapped with high doses of radioactivity. She could not see anybody, although she could hear my voice from behind the lead protective shielding. I talked to her constantly. On the way back we passed a drinks machine and, inevitably, Gemma demanded some money to put in it. The sister who was with us said that would be impossible, but I forced the porter to stop and Gemma got her way. We made six trips to the radiotherapy room in all, and Gemma put some money in the machine on the way back every time. On the final visit, fed up with the hospital, she decided to make a fuss. She refused to keep still in the darkened room and just kept screaming. Amy's parents, Denise and Steven, were with me behind the shielding, and we all started singing rude songs. They may have sounded odd, but they succeeded in quietening Gemma down.

I had to argue for Gemma to be allowed to return to the Royal Victoria Infirmary in her own clothes. After another short ambulance journey with everyone in gowns and masks, we arrived back to Gemma's room to find it had been thoroughly scrubbed. The red sticky tape on the floor had been moved a little to try and give her more space, and all the nurses were there to welcome her back. Inside the red line, Gemma refused to let anyone catch her to reconnect her to a drip by dodging from one side to the other. One of us had to gown up and hold her down. She could not stop laughing, she was so pleased to be back.

Steven, meanwhile, having fought off a chest infection with the aid of antibiotics, was having his bone marrow sucked out for the third time. This time he recovered well. When it came to syringing his marrow into Gemma's long line, she asked the doctor if she could do it. 'If you want something doing properly, do it yourself,' she said. 'My Mam always says that.' Gemma put on a pair of surgical gloves and slowly squeezed in Steven's yellow matter. Everyone cheered, lots of photographs were taken, and it was Day I again.

I had to go home for a few days to recover from a mild infection. When my father brought me back, he gave Gemma a £20 note which she put in the zip pocket of her hat. Then, at around three o'clock in the morning, I was woken by the news that Gemma was demanding my presence in her room. She was sitting up in bed looking through a mail order catalogue, and told me she wanted a tea set. I am afraid that I lost my temper and yelled at her. She immediately started to cry, and I washed and gowned up as quickly as I could. 'I'm sorry Gemma, I didn't mean to shout. I'm just so tired,' I said. She told me she was miserable and wanted to go home. I promised that, whatever happened, she would indeed go home when this transplant was over.

Having gowned up, I went over the red line and we shed more tears together.

'Can I have a Mackie tomorrow, Mam?' she asked when she had calmed down. 'That's why I want the tea set.' I had to laugh and say yes – as long as she did not tell anyone else, as it was still meant to be forbidden. So I went out and bought her a blue china tea set, which she loved. When no one else was about I slipped her a small can of Mackie, and she carefully poured it into one of the cups. When the doctor came round she politely offered him the cup, saying it was black coffee. Thankfully, he refused.

On Day 13 of the third transplant, after a number of now familiar problems with skin rashes and sickness, one of the doctors called me into her office to tell me the latest blood count. Although overall it was still 0.2, she was excited because it showed that neutrophils, one of the most important types of white blood cells for fighting infection, had reached a level of 46 per cent. This had not happened before and suggested that something might be starting to happen in Gemma's bone marrow. Steven and I refused to get excited, having had our hopes dashed too often in the past. On the same day, Gary, the boy opposite, was having his air flow turned off because his transplant seemed to have been successful. Gemma was cross because he had been there for a much shorter time than she had. She consoled herself with the inevitable Mackie and we shut the door to drown out the cheers and clapping as his ventilation machine was switched off.

On Day 14 – 121 days after Gemma was first admitted – we had the best news so far. Her count rose to 0.4, her neutrophils to 53 per cent, and she seemed very well. 'Don't know whether to get the flags out or not, but can't wait until tomorrow's count,' I wrote in the diary. 'But I've said that before somewhere.' On Day 15 the neutrophils dropped to 33 per cent but the white blood count rose again to 0.6 – the highest since treatment had begun. 'Can see some light at the end of the tunnel,' records the diary. On Day 16 the count reached 1.0 for the first time and on Day 17 it was 1.5. It was getting difficult to contain our euphoria.

Unfortunately Gemma herself seemed quite ill some of the time, partly due to an infection and partly because her sleeping pattern had been disturbed to such an extent that she was mixing up night and day. On Day 18 – Monday, 14 May 1990 – we were having a break in the coffee room with Steven's parents when one of the nurses from the ward rang to tell me the latest results. Gemma's white blood count was up to 2.7, with 71 per cent neutrophils. Trying to contain our excitement, we rushed back to the ward, where we were met by one of the doctors. He told us that the transplant was obviously working and Gemma could come out of her red-line prison.

When we told her, she did not believe us and refused to step over the line. 'I need a mask,' she said.

'You don't any more,' we told her. 'You're better.'

But still she refused to come out, so deeply ingrained were the habits and fears of the last four months. I had to walk across the line, unmasked and with no gown, and hold her hand before she could finally be persuaded to take a few tentative steps into the rest of her life. Steven showed her the big red button which switched off the air flow and, to loud cheers, she pressed it off. Then she bent down and started deliberately tearing up the sticky red tape that had defined her life for so long. When one of the nurses bent down to wish her well, she stuck it on his chin. 'Just want to be left on our own. Could be home a week on Friday hopefully,' says the diary.

On Day 19 Steven and I got permission to take her for a short walk in the nearby park in a wheelchair. It was rainy but she thought it was wonderful. She fed the ducks, felt the breeze and slept for hours afterwards. 'Just cannot put into words how Susan and I are feeling,' said Steven in the diary. The only problem we had was trying to prevent her from tiring herself out by trying to do too much. On Day 22, with her blood count remaining stable, she grabbed hold of the diary and wrote in large infant scrawl: 'I HAVE BEEN IN HOSPITAL FOR LONG TIME.' On Day 23 she turned up in a wheelchair at the door to the parents' room early in the morning, before Steven and I had left, announcing that she was going to make us a cup of tea. A shamefaced nurse who was with her, described how she had tricked a porter into allowing her to escape from the ward. The nurse had found her halfway along the corridor and tried to persuade her to turn around, but she had rebelled. She had put her fingers through the spokes of her wheelchair and refused to remove them unless she was taken to our room.

With the aid of a huge chart, we started to assume responsibility for giving Gemma all her pills. On Day 24 we told the hospital we were going off for the day and would be back in the evening. We put Gemma in the back of the car and, for the first time in more than four months, drove home. We turned up unannounced at Tina's, much to her surprise, and had a wonderful lunch with her, Bianca, Richenda and my father. We showed Gemma how we had redecorated her bedroom, and paid another surprise visit on Steven's parents. His mother nearly collapsed with shock, totally unable to control her emotions. The last people we saw before we drove back to Newcastle were Helen's identical twins from next door, whom Gemma used to play with all the time. Because they had not seen her since she went into hospital, they were a little scared of the cap covering her bald head. Then she did something strange to break the ice. She took off her cap and placed one of their hands on her head. 'Feel it,' she said. 'It's like a baby's bottom.'

On Day 29 the doctors said that Gemma might be able to go home the following day. Steven and I went out for a meal with some of the other parents on the ward. We got back late, but were woken after only an hour to be told that Gemma was being sick. When I got to her she looked very pale, and I could not make out what it was she was throwing up. The nurse told me it was milk shake. When I asked where on earth she could have got that from, the nurse informed me that it had come with the pizzas. It turned out that Gemma had used her mobile telephone to order pizzas to be delivered to her and the boy in the next bed, and they had wolfed the lot. By good fortune, Gemma was able to pay for them because she still had the £20 that my father had given her stashed away in the zip pocket of her hat.

Because of her sickness and then a raised temperature, her return home had to be frustratingly postponed for a few days while she finished a course of antibiotics. I took the chance to return the mobile telephone to the British Telecom shop, along with a framed photograph of Gemma using it. I was never charged a single penny for the hire, nor for any of the hundreds of calls that Gemma had made, for which I could not thank British Telecom enough.

It was not until Day 35 that the infection finally cleared up and we were at last told that we could go home. A mother on the ward presented us with a portable electronic blood pressure gauge so that I could check Gemma's blood without calling on a nurse. Gemma bought all the doctors and nurses a gift each and a large tin of chocolate biscuits to eat with their tea. Then, just after lunch on Thursday, 31 May 1990 – 143 days since we had first arrived – we walked out, our hearts full of hope for the future.

Chapter 9

Fairground in the Sky

'NUCLEAR TIME-BOMB GIRL GEMMA SAVED' was the headline in the *Daily Mirror*. 'Courageous little Gemma D'Arcy last night won her desperate fight for life against a "nuclear timebomb" killer,' said the story underneath. 'Jubilant doctors revealed that the brave six-year-old has beaten leukaemia after a third – and final – bone marrow transplant from her dad Steve.' I was quoted as saying that we were 'absolutely thrilled and very relieved'. Other newspapers ran similar stories, and Gemma and I made a couple of television appearances. It was all true: those were good days.

When we arrived back in Cleator Moor from Newcastle, there were balloons and a 'Welcome Home' poster in our local shop. Outside our front door hung a huge banner greeting Gemma, and there were dozens of balloons all over the place. The neighbours, who had clubbed together to buy us a huge bouquet of flowers, all came out to greet us. Afterwards we spent a quiet evening in the house, watching television and eating a Chinese meal, until it was time for Gemma to go and sleep in her own bed. In the middle of the night I was awakened by footsteps. Through my bedroom door I watched as Richenda took Gemma carefully by the hand to the toilet. It was a sight that made me want to weep for joy.

It was almost too good to be true to be home again doing the simple things that families do, looking forward to simple pleasures, but it was scary too. Gemma's immune system was still damaged, her blood count was not completely back to normal and she tired very easily. She was still bald and her face was terribly puffed up from the drugs, half-closing her eyes. We still had to protect her from the risk of even the mildest infection, such as cold sores, which meant restricting the children with whom she could play. I was terrified that I would forget to give her one of her fourteen different drugs at the right time. We were never long away from hospitals because of all the blood transfusions, check-ups and follow-up treatment which were necessary. The first full day we were back, we had to go to the local hospital to get a transfusion of platelets as Gemma's new bone marrow was not yet producing them. I became so impatient with the slow rate at which the drip was being fed into Gemma's long line that I turned it up and finished the job myself, something they let me repeat on subsequent visits.

Our first return visit to the Royal Victoria Infirmary in Newcastle was just five days after we had left. Gemma's white blood count had topped 4 – the best yet – and the doctors seemed very pleased with her progress. There were sunny days when Gemma played in the garden on the swing, skipped or helped Steven with the weeding. In the evenings she was often very hungry, talkative and effervescent. On the second weekend at home Denise and Steven came across from Newcastle. We drove to Ennerdale in the Lake District, had a picnic and walked around the lake at dusk, gazing at the hillsides. Gemma was full of life and loved it. On Sunday it was very hot and we had a barbecue in the back garden. On the Monday, Steven started back at work at Sellafield. Things began to feel almost normal again.

Then, four days later, after another blood transfusion, Gemma suddenly took a turn for the worse. She was vomiting and had bad diarrhoea. By the time we arrived at the hospital in Newcastle she was having difficulty breathing, her lips looked blue and she needed oxygen. The doctors told us that she had developed graft versus host disease, a common and sometimes serious complication of bone marrow transplants. Steven's bone marrow was rejecting Gemma's cells as alien. We were warned that this might require a lung biopsy and a period in intensive care, although thankfully we avoided both. But Gemma did have to stay in hospital for another long and anxious three weeks before she was allowed home again. Even then she still had a mild form of the disease and the trips to hospital for tests, check-ups and transfusions seemed endless.

Gemma became very depressed and withdrawn. All she seemed to want to do was to visit the shops, either to spend money or to watch people spending money. It became quite difficult to get a smile out of her, although there were flashes of the old Gemma now and again. On one occasion she came back from the shops with a half bottle of sparkling wine for Steven and a packet of sanitary towels for me. She seemed to lose interest in eating, shed a lot of weight and began to look very frail. Walking became increasingly painful, and she complained that her legs hurt. I had this vision of her bones beginning to crumble inside her body. She was put on morphine again to ease the pain, and the doctors recommended swimming. I took her to the pool as often as I could, because it was one of the few things she still seemed to enjoy.

The doctors told me that her depression could be due to the radiation treatment and she should snap out of it soon. They suggested restarting Gemma at school for a couple of mornings a week and said they would get in touch with the education authority. Sometimes, when I was feeling particularly frayed, I could not help losing my temper at her and shouting. Of course I always felt guilty afterwards and often became emotional. One evening at home Gemma, Richenda and I were all watching television while Steven was cooking our tea. Gemma asked for another pair of new shoes and I said we would see. Richenda started loudly complaining about how Gemma got everything and she got nothing. She burst into tears, causing Gemma and then me to do the same. Gemma hated being accused of being spoilt, Richenda was full of jealousy, and I knew that Richenda would only really understand when it was too late. After lots of shouting and tears, we all said sorry to each other and started laughing at something on the television.

One day we were out shopping and Gemma lighted on an expensive black velvet dress with royal blue satin puff sleeves and a ridiculous bow which I thought did not suit her at all. The shop allowed us to take it home for her to try on, and Steven promised to buy it for her. Gemma rang my father and asked him for £10 towards a new pair of shoes to go with it, which she bought the next day. As she was parading around the house in her new outfit, she suddenly started screaming about pains in her back. Complete with her dress, we drove her over to Newcastle as soon as we could so that the doctors could adjust the morphine dose, which took a couple of days. At night I slept with Gemma on the ward and was wakened by her shouting for a nurse. I pretended to be asleep while she commanded the nurse to make me a cup of tea before I woke up. All morning she sat on her bed, bald, in her new dress and shoes looking like the Queen of Sheba. When we drove home with Steven, she had just been given a large morphine tablet. She said she felt drunk and it was lovely.

We had a visit from the local director of education and then the primary school headmistress to discuss the arrangements for Gemma returning to school. She was looking forward to it, and Steven and I were hoping that mixing with other children might help cheer her up. It was agreed that I should stay with her for the first few occasions. Gemma, meanwhile, kept feeling sick, so on one of our regular visits to the local hospital she took some anti-sickness drugs. On the way back in the car, she still felt ill and looked miserable. As we pulled up outside the house, I turned round and asked her how she felt. 'I feel like I'm dying, Mam,' she replied. I said nothing for ten seconds and then told her not to be silly – she would feel better later.

Three days before Gemma was due to start school, I went out with her blessing to play in a darts match at our local pub. When I got back, she shouted from her bedroom to ask if I had won. I told her I had not and went up to see her. She asked me to clean out her ears, told me she loved me and went to sleep. With Steven and Russell, I then ate a superb meal of peppered steak, bacon and sauté potatoes with garlic. We talked optimistically about Gemma's future at school. Steven suggested that I should have a rare lie-in the next morning while he looked after Gemma and made sure she took the right drugs.

In the morning I woke late. Gemma, still in her pyjamas, was sitting listlessly on the sofa in the living room and breathing heavily. Steven said she had been like that all morning and he had failed to get any reading on the blood pressure monitor, which I assumed meant it was broken. I arranged to take her to the local hospital at once to get her checked over. 'I don't want to go to hospital, Mam,' she said. 'I'm sorry I spoiled your morning off.' In the car her condition seemed to deteriorate. She kept apologising for feeling ill and promising to get better soon. At the hospital, by a strange coincidence we saw the same doctor who had initially diagnosed Gemma three years previously, Dr Roberts. He had retired in the interim, but was on duty that day standing in for someone else. I took a blood sample from Gemma's long line and, while we waited for the analysis to come back, Dr Roberts tried to examine Gemma. She kept screaming at him because she was frightened he would hurt her as he had the first time.

The aim was to assess whether Gemma was fit enough to travel over to Newcastle for a full examination. Dr Roberts had organised an ambulance to take us, but when the results of the blood test arrived it emerged that Gemma's potassium count was very low. This meant that she would have to have a potassium infusion before she travelled, a process that usually took about an hour. She lay on a bed with a drip and complained that her legs were aching. Steven and I took it in turns to rub them, as she dozed. A nurse came and tried to measure her blood pressure but, like Steven earlier, could not get a reading. She thought it must be due to the arm cuff she was using, so tried again with another one. This time she managed to get a reading, but it was dangerously low. I began to realise that Gemma was seriously ill, and getting worse.

I started trying to ring Tina but kept getting no answer. Gemma's lips turned blue and Dr Roberts gave her some oxygen, which she resisted at first but then enjoyed. She said she felt very hot inside and kept asking for iced drinks, which a nurse supplied. She was very anxious about how we would manage to provide cold drinks during the ambulance ride to Newcastle, but much comforted by the nurse's suggestion that we could take a thermos flask. I eventually managed to reach Tina and she and Russell appeared almost at once. We all took it in turns to keep rubbing Gemma's legs. She seemed less and less aware of what was happening, drifting in and out of consciousness. I could tell by the way that the doctors were looking at each other that they were growing alarmed. When a nurse asked me whether I would like a priest in attendance, I began to fear that she was going to die. Clinging to hope, I refused.

A doctor asked me quickly to remove the bung from Gemma's line so that he could give her an emergency blood transfusion. He filled up a syringe with blood straight from the drip bag hanging at Gemma's side. I started putting on sterile gloves, but then realised the urgency of the situation and just tore out the bung with my bare hands. He pumped the blood directly into Gemma's veins, but it did not seem to do any good. The nurse asked me again if I would like a priest and this time I nodded, with tears rolling down my cheeks. I telephoned my father and Steven's parents, who all arrived as soon as they could. I watched, unbelieving, as the priest administered the last rites to Gemma.

She fell into a coma from which the doctors thought it unlikely that she would ever awake. Then an extraordinary thing happened. We were all in the room talking to her as she lay unconscious on the bed, when she suddenly opened her eyes and raised herself up a little. She stared past everyone towards the corner of the room, smiled and lay back down again to sleep.

It was then that Dr Roberts decided that Gemma should be transferred to intensive care. Steven argued against this at first because he wanted her to die in peace. I begged him to allow it, pointing out that we had seen other children in the leukaemia ward recover after intensive care. He relented and Gemma was rushed up five floors in a lift, while we all ran up the stairs. The staff would not allow us into the intensive care unit for about three-quarters of an hour while Gemma was being connected up to a life support machine. I was worried that they might be hurting her. When we were eventually allowed in, we saw her lying on a furry mattress wrapped in bright tin foil to help her retain body heat. There were wires coming out of her everywhere, and a large black tube in her mouth that seemed to be breathing for her. She looked calm and relaxed, which made me feel better.

I went round the side of her bed, put my hand under the tin foil and started rubbing her legs as she had liked us doing downstairs.

Even though she did not look as if she was in pain, I angrily insisted that she should be given some morphine just in case. A nurse told us that she might be able to hear what we were saying. Steven took over rubbing her legs and I held her hand. Staring closely at her face, I saw a single tear roll across her cheek as if she was still saying sorry for becoming ill and causing us all this heartache. 'Don't cry, Gemma. We are all here and we love you,' I whispered.

In between sitting with Gemma I wandered around the intensive care ward. I talked to a bedridden old man and told him to hang on and fight. I watched as a young man was treated for a deliberate drugs overdose, and felt very angry that he should have tried to end his life when my Gemma was fighting desperately for hers in the next room. I organised a constant flow of friends and relatives to say goodbye to her, trying to warn them how strange and ill she looked. I heard one of them screaming alone in the toilet. I explained as best I could to Richenda what was happening and left her alone with Gemma for a few minutes. She came out looking calm, but with tears in her eyes.

Shortly after two o'clock in the morning, a doctor examining Gemma expressed some surprise. He told me that her kidneys seemed to be functioning, her blood pressure had improved and her blood count had increased. 'If she carries on like this,' he said, 'we may be able to take her out of intensive care in two or three days.' With some tiny hope rekindled, Steven and I experienced a huge surge of relief. Leaving Tina and Russell at her bedside, we decided to try and get some sleep so that we would be strong for Gemma in the morning. We explained to her what we were doing, told her to keep up the good work, and kissed her goodnight.

Stupidly, the only beds the hospital was able to provide for us were two long corridors and five flights of stairs away. Steven eventually fell asleep on his camp bed, but I just stared into the darkness with a million memories of Gemma swirling round my brain. I had no idea what the time was when a nurse appeared and told me to come because Gemma had taken a turn for the worse. I stepped over Steven and walked along the corridor, feeling that there was no point in rushing. In the lift was one of the doctors who had attended Gemma earlier, wearing his pyjamas under his white coat. We did not speak. When the lift doors opened, a nurse was standing there crying. She went to put her arms around me, but I jumped back. Trying to control her emotions, she said: 'She died five minutes ago.'

Tina later told me exactly what had happened. Gemma had never regained consciousness. Some time before dawn, her heart machine started becoming erratic. A nurse, desperately trying to keep her alive, said she was losing her fast. Tina, holding her limp body in her arms, begged her to wait for her Mam to come. Every time Tina spoke, the dials on the machines flickered as if Gemma was still listening. She seemed to be struggling to hang on for me. Tina, realising that I was going to arrive too late, told a lie. 'It's all right Gemma, your Mam's here. You can go now.' It was five minutes to six on Sunday, 23 September 1990. She was six years and ten months old.

I stood at the end of her bed and gazed at her. It looked like she was still breathing because the machine was still on. 'Bye, Gemma,' I said. 'I love you.' I moved closer and looked at her face. In the corner of her eye there was another tear. 'Don't be sorry, Gemma. It's about time you let go. Now you can go to your fairground in the sky and wait there for the rest of us.'

I hope to God she is still waiting.

Chapter 10

She Wore Blue Velvet

'Why?' The sound of the word roared out of Steven's lungs and echoed round the mountainsides. It was a roar of pure pain, a roar of unforgiving anger, a desolate roar of inconsolable grief. He was standing on the top of a large rock in Wasdale, by the shore of Wastwater in the tranquil heart of the Lake District. I was standing nearby, watching and weeping. We had driven for hours in silence, parked near the lake and walked over to a grassy bank overlooking a tiny pebbled beach. I remember the scree slopes towering high over the water, little waves lapping gently on the shore, and people the size of ants walking up the huge hillsides. I remember the silence that preceded Steven's roar and the silence that followed in its wake. I remember the words that Steven then started repeating over and over again, as if he was trying to convince himself that they were true. 'This place is beautiful, Susan, but our Gemma will never see it.'

The few days that immediately followed her death were full of such intense, defining moments. All my senses seemed to be heightened, so that I perceived otherwise ordinary events with a clarity and potency that rendered them unforgettable. I shall certainly never forget driving home from the hospital with no one in the back of the car. The silence was so strange that Steven turned on the radio. Someone was singing about the dress she wore being made of 'Blue Velvet'. We looked at each other, thought of Gemma's last extravagant purchase a few days ago, and cried. When the undertaker asked us what Gemma should wear in her coffin, we had no choice but her ridiculous new velvet dress and shoes. When we thought about the music we should play at her funeral, the song chose itself.

There was a great deal of sadness and an irreconcilable feeling of loss. Steven and I talked through the night about our feelings. He felt guilty about giving Gemma the bone marrow that eventually killed her. I felt guilty about going out to the pub darts match two nights before she died. We both felt irrationally angry with the school for failing to admit her sooner, and furious at the hospital for failing to predict and prevent her final relapse. At times we simply could not believe what had happened. I remember waking up the first morning after her death and thinking it had all been a horrendous nightmare. It was not until I had checked Gemma's bedroom and found it empty that I fully recalled the reality. There were two memorable occasions when the tension became so great that I cracked and started to yell, once at my Dad and once at Steven.

There was also, although I still feel guilty admitting it, an occasionally overwhelming feeling of relief. With no drugs to administer, no blood pressure to take, no constant care to give, I sometimes felt as if I was on holiday. The nightmare through which we had all been living for the last three years had at last come to an end. The endless gnawing uncertainty, the huge roller-coasters of hope and despair, the eternal agony of ignorance had been replaced by something final, something indisputable, something for ever immutable. Gemma's suffering – thank God – was over.

Only the constant, frenetic blur of activity dulled our feelings. We spoke on the telephone to dozens of people – relatives, old friends in Cumbria, the new friends we had made in Newcastle, the school, the church, Martyn Day, the local and national media. We made arrangements with the undertaker for Gemma to lie in a parlour of rest, planned the funeral and told the priest about the angel and the devil that was our Gemma. As well as Tina and the rest of the family, we were very lucky to have the help and support of many good friends. We hardly ever seemed to be alone, with people calling round to see us all the time. Although I did not ask them, Amy's mother, Denise, and our friend Alison drove over from Newcastle to be with us, which was wonderful. We got scores of lovely cards and letters, including a special 'Airmail' one to Gemma in heaven from Bianca. People from all walks of life who had met Gemma took the trouble to write, including fund-raisers, bone marrow campaigners, journalists, television producers and hospital staff. Dr Jenny Kernahan sent a moving letter, as did other staff who had helped look after Gemma during her long stay in hospital. One nurse told us that someone had written in Ward 16 South's news book: 'Is there life after Gemma D'Arcy?'

Immediately after Gemma's life support machine had been turned off and her chest had ceased being artificially pumped up and down, we were asked by the hospital if we would permit a post-mortem. We agreed, on the understanding that the knowledge gained about how she died could be used to help other children in the future. I would have donated her kidneys for someone else to use, but they had been too damaged by her disease. The thought that some small benefit might come of Gemma's death gave us strength. Her death certificate said that she had died because of 'Septicaemia due to leukaemia'. According to the dictionary, septicaemia means 'the presence of pathogenic bacteria in the blood'. The way I see it, her beautiful little body, racked for more than three years with a disease that destroyed her blood, bombarded with huge amounts of toxic drugs and radiation, then forced to accept some alien tissue, finally gave up the ghost. Its immune system fatally damaged, it allowed into her blood a poison which killed her.

I have one regret, though, about the post-mortem, and that relates to Richenda. She was the one I was most worried about after Gemma's death. I felt that Steven and I had in some obscure but fundamental way let her down by allowing her sister to die. We tried as best we could to comfort her, but she was only ten and found it hard to cope. The first night she could not get to sleep at all, so we put her into our bed. She just lay there and cried. She told me that she was terribly scared because she thought that she would be next to die. I told her that this was nonsense. I said Gemma was all right because her soul had gone to heaven. All that was left down here on earth was her shell. She had abandoned her shell that night in the hospital. I suggested Richenda close her eyes. 'What can you see, Shenda?' I asked.

'Nothing,' she replied.

'That's because the real you, your soul, is inside and your eyes are windows to the world. Your skin, your outside, is like a raincoat that keeps you dry. It's really no more than a shell. Some people like you are lucky and get really beautiful shells. Others get really ugly shells.' Richenda laughed, turned over and went to sleep.

When Gemma was laid in the parlour of rest, I could not at first face going to see her. Perhaps it was irrational, but I was worried that the post-mortem might have somehow changed her appearance. Richenda, though, was keen to go and Tina, who had already been, agreed to take her. When Richenda returned, she looked pale. She did not say much about it at the time, but four years later she described what had happened:

> It was awful, the worst thing of all, just seeing her lying there, not moving. She was wearing her favourite dress: black velvet round the neck with a flared blue satin skirt. It was a really dreadful dress but she loved it. She had on her purple and black party shoes that she'd persuaded Grandad to buy her. I stood there silently, just looking. Something made me lift up her dress to see if she had knickers on, because I did not want her to be embarrassed without them. There were staples along her leg. I ran out shouting: 'That's not Gemma.' It was horrible.

I decided I had to go too. My father drove Steven and me to the funeral parlour, which was right next door to the comprehensive school which I used to go to, and to which Richenda would go. There were lots of children running around shouting, all very alive. Gemma was lying in the first of three rooms off a small waiting area. Steven and I slowly walked in and there was our girl, quite still but looking for all the world as if she was just asleep. By her side was Butch, her cuddly toy bulldog, and a bobble for her hair which one of my friends had put in because he had promised to give her one for when her hair grew back. Steven put in some money in case she needed any for the fairground in the sky. I thought she looked very elegant in her dress, although I could see some sticky tape on her legs underneath her knee socks. I was quite calm until I saw the coffin lid with its small gold-plated plaque: 'Gemma D'Arcy 1983–1990.' The thought of the lid being screwed down began to disturb me. I imagined how dark it would be. As Steven bent over and kissed her goodbye, I began to cry. After we walked out, he said he regretted that last kiss, the memory of which will stay with him for ever. 'She was so cold,' he said.

The evening before the funeral, Denise and her husband, Steven, came over from Newcastle and stayed the night, for which I was very grateful. Having lost their baby girl, Amy, no more than six months earlier, they knew more than anyone what Steven and I were going through. We just talked and talked: about Gemma, about Amy, about the hospital and about our feelings. Their company that night was more valued than I can ever say.

For the funeral we had asked the priest if we could do something unconventional. I wanted Gemma cremated, but I also wanted her ashes buried with a headstone which people could visit. We had a service in a church – St Mary's in Cleator Moor – and another in a crematorium, choosing our own music and one of our own singers. We wanted to make it a farewell that everyone would remember.

Instead of black, I put on a bright and colourful dress which Gemma loved. It was a beautiful, sunny morning and people started arriving at our house at about half-past eight. I looked out of the window and was amazed to see how many people there were: friends and everyone from both sides of the family, including some I did not even recognise. I went outside to say thank you to everyone, my heart bursting with pride for Gemma. She was so young, yet such a fighter. She had endured so much because of our decision to try the three bone marrow transplants, but she had never blamed us. Then the flowers started to arrive: simple posies, extravagant arrangements, wreaths large and small. My aunties from Italy had sent a floral 'Heaven's Gate' and there were floral teddy bears, floral Worzel Gummidges and – from Tina – Gemma's name spelt out in large floral letters. When the funeral cars came into sight, I couldn't stop myself shouting out: 'Steven, she's home.'

At the church, I had to stop Steven doing physical damage to a television camera crew which was filming people arriving. Gemma's coffin was put on a trolley and wheeled in with us following behind. I was again overwhelmed with pride when I saw the pews packed with people. As well as family and friends, there were many members of the local community who knew her; Sellafield workers who had helped raise money to send her to Disneyland; thirty-one children from her school, St Patrick's; the teachers who had taught her; the doctors who had tried to save her; the nurses who had tended her; the journalists who had written about her; the relatives of other leukaemia victims in the area who were part of the legal action; the lawyers who were representing us all in court; and many, many more. After the hymns, the schoolchildren sang 'All things bright and beautiful', which had been Gemma's favourite. At the end Steve Falcon, the singer who had done so much to help send Gemma to Disneyland, stood up and sang the song that had become her theme tune during the fund-raising: Nat King Cole's 'When I Fall in Love'. I think everyone in the church except me was in tears. My tears were all cried out.

After the service everyone went to the crematorium, where there was a very short ceremony. When the coffin disappeared behind the curtains, I started to giggle to myself. I had a powerful vision of Gemma dancing about and pulling faces behind the curtain, laughing at us all sitting there so solemnly. As we were walking out, 'Blue Velvet' starting playing and Steven and I smiled at each other.

> But in my heart there'll always be
> Precious and warm, a memory
> Through the years
> And I can still see blue velvet
> Through my tears.

In Helen's pub later, where we held the wake, Gemma's funeral appeared all over again on the television in the bar next door. I was upset at first, but then I thought it gave the thousands of people who had known about Gemma but could not have come to her funeral their chance to mourn.

Gemma's actual burial in the churchyard was a small, simple, family affair and very moving. On her tombstone we put her picture and wrote:

Treasured Memories
of
GEMMA D'ARCY
who died
23rd September 1990
aged six years ten months
beloved daughter of
Susan and Steven
and dear sister to
Richenda
Life like a Butterfly

After the funeral of one child, you do not expect another. Helen has always been one of my best friends in Cleator Moor. Her daughter, Kerry, was a friend of Richenda's and had shared birthday parties with Gemma. Helen was always there for me through the hard times, and she was one of the first people we went to see the morning of Gemma's death. I vividly remember her standing in the kitchen explaining to Kerry, who was still in her pyjamas, what had happened. 'We won't be celebrating your birthday this year,' she said, at which Kerry had just nodded silently in agreement.

One morning about a week later, I saw Kerry again. Waiting in the car across the street from Helen's house to pick up one of her neighbours to go to work, I caught sight of Kerry leaving home on her way to school. She saw me and waved as she closed her door. I remember thinking how odd it was that she was not wearing her school uniform.

That afternoon, I got a call at work from Tina. She told me to go immediately to Helen's house because something was wrong. I drove there as fast as I could, cursing all the slow-motion traffic and pedestrians that seemed to impede my progress. The weather was appalling: raining, icy cold and blowing a gale. When I arrived, Helen flung her arms around me, crying. She told me between sobs that Kerry was missing. She had not been wearing her school uniform that morning because she had been going on the school's sponsored walk. On the way home she had stopped by the edge of a river to wash her boots, slipped and fallen in. The river, swollen by the rain into a raging torrent, had swept her away downstream. They had to search for three days before they found her body. She was eleven years old.

Two months later, when it would have been Gemma's and Kerry's birthdays, one of the nurses from the Royal Victoria Infirmary in Newcastle sent me a beautiful poem. It was written by Christina Rossetti more than a hundred years ago.

> Remember me when I am gone away,
> Gone far away into the silent land;
> When you can no more hold me by the hand,
> Nor I half turn to go yet turning stay.
> Remember me when no more day by day
> You tell me of our future that you planned:
> Only remember me; you understand
> It will be late to counsel then or pray.
> Yet if you should forget me for a while
> And afterwards remember, do not grieve:
> For if the darkness and corruption leave
> A vestige of the thoughts that once I had,
> Better by far you should forget and smile
> Than that you should remember and be sad.

Chapter 11

One of Many

The second morning after Gemma's death, Steven, Richenda and I drove to one of the beaches near Sellafield. We walked to the stony end of the bay where there were no people and sat down. Without warning, Richenda suddenly stood up and started throwing stones into the sea. 'Why Gemma? Why did she have to die?' she shouted with all the unrestrained anger of a ten-year-old. Steven started silently throwing stones too, while I just sat and stared out to sea. I was channelling my aggression in another direction. Gemma had loved this beach and we had come there to play often. But I did not really know why we were there thirty hours after she had died. I hated the place. I loathed it. I knew that the whole shoreline had been polluted by Sellafield: radiation in the sand, poison in the salt spray, plutonium in the sea. I could almost taste the contamination on my tongue. I was sure that it had something to do with Gemma's leukaemia. I was certain it had contributed to her death. It was then that I made the decision that has determined the rest of my life. There was no way I would ever give up fighting for Gemma.

The period immediately after the formal mourning was the worst. Deprived of ceremony, of the constant coming and going of people, of the concern of many, we just had to carry on. Richenda went back to school. Despite all that had happened, Steven went back to work for a contractor at Sellafield. That may seem like a crazy thing to have done, but it was the only place where he could realistically get a job, and we desperately needed the money. In any case the moral dilemma did not last long, because he only worked at Sellafield for another six months before he was transferred somewhere else and then made redundant.

I was left on my own in the house, which seemed so quiet without Gemma. I missed her with a pain that was physical. Friends and relatives gave me tremendous support, but I decided I had to get a job to prevent me getting seriously depressed. The first factory I went to offered me work the moment they realised that I was Gemma's mother, which upset me because I wanted to be chosen on my merit and not because I used to have a famous daughter. I started doing a few shifts instead at my aunty's packaging factory nearby, but I never really settled down to anything. For the first twelve months after Gemma's death, I must have worked in at least eight different places.

The one purpose that did inspire me, that kept me going, was the legal action against British Nuclear Fuels. I was in regular touch with Martyn Day, and whenever I got the opportunity to talk about Gemma on the television or in the newspapers I took it. Because of the publicity that the legal action continued to attract, there were frequent opportunities. Some people suggested to me that now Gemma was dead I should stop fighting, but I took the opposite view. All I had left were photographs, videotapes, a scrapbook and my memories, but I was more than ever determined that she should not have died in vain. I wanted to make sure that she would never be forgotten. I wanted to talk about her, about what she was like, about how she suffered and about why I blamed Sellafield. I wanted the world to think twice about nuclear power. Which was more important: power, profit and jobs, or the lives of innocent children?

So when Martyn told me that Granada Television were interested in making a hard-hitting drama-documentary using actors to tell the story behind the court cases, I got involved. I let my rooms and windows be measured so that our house could be recreated on a film set in Manchester. I talked to the producers, Ian McBride and Sita Williams, for hours about Gemma, what she was like and everything that had happened to her. I lent them lots of personal photographs and videotapes. I suggested that Tina's daughter, Bianca, be cast in the part of Gemma (which after two auditions she nearly was). I went along to the first audition, took offence at the off-hand attitude of one of Granada's senior staff and was stupidly rude to some of the parents when they started worrying about their children's hair being cut off to resemble Gemma. I angrily insisted that Steven's father be left out of the documentary as I did not want to risk offending him again. I tried to tell Lorraine Ashbourne, the actress who was going to play me, what I was like – as did Steven with Gary Mavers, the actor who was going to play him. I once went to watch them filming on the beach, but the effect of seeing Jennifer Kate Wilson, the little girl from Workington who was eventually chosen to play Gemma, limping towards the car wearing an over-sized jacket and a baseball cap just like Gemma's was too much to handle. I never watched them filming again.

As Martyn Day and his team delved deeper into the background to the legal action, they decided that Gemma was no longer going to be one of the front-line test cases. Their reasoning was that the most likely way to win the case was to hinge it on Professor Gardner's new evidence linking the exposure of fathers to high radiation doses at Sellafield with the incidence of leukaemia amongst their children. The connection was particularly strong where fathers had received more than 100 millisieverts (a measure of radiation dose) prior to conception. The problem with our case, apparently, was that there was no firm evidence that Steven had ever been exposed to such high levels of radiation. According to BNFL's records, he had only received a dose of 9.11 millisieverts between 1977 and 1983, the period before Gemma was conceived. The fathers of the two chosen test cases – George Reay, whose daughter Dorothy had died of leukaemia when she was ten months old, and David Hope, whose daughter Vivien was left permanently disabled after recovering from a disease closely related to leukaemia – both had much higher recorded radiation doses (384 and 184 millisieverts respectively).

Although I was disappointed by the decision, I accepted it. Steven had sometimes been employed in areas which BNFL classed as 'non-active' and had therefore not always been issued with a radiation badge. Even when he did wear a badge, he had doubts about its reliability. It was therefore impossible to say what levels he had actually been exposed to. I could also not rule out another possibility: that it was not just Steven's irradiation that had caused Gemma's death, but the radioactive contamination of the environment outside Sellafield. I kept thinking about all those days we played on the beach and how easy it would have been to have inadvertently picked up something that sparked off the malfunction in Gemma's bone marrow.

In their investigations Martyn and his team managed to unearth some damning evidence about BNFL's past practices at Sellafield. They discovered, for example, that the radiation badges worn in the 1950s and early 1960s were systematically underestimating the levels of radiation to which workers were actually exposed by as much as 50 per cent. The information was revealed in a four-page paper found within one of the huge piles of documents which BNFL were forced to release by the court. Written in August 1960 by Sellafield's head of health and safety, Huw Howells, it recommended that a note should be added to workers' dose records explaining that they were significant underestimates. His recommendation, however, was ignored and no such note ever appeared. That meant that all the dose records that formed the basis of Professor Gardner's report were too low. It also meant that the dose levels recorded for George Reay and David Hope were too low. By the time their cases came to court, this was a point that BNFL had conceded. George Reay's real lifetime dose, the company admitted, was more than one and a half times higher that that recorded on his official records (639 instead of 384 millisieverts). He died of cancer in the mid-1980s, for which his wife, Elizabeth, blamed Sellafield.

What Martyn's team discovered about radiation releases into the environment from Sellafield was, to my mind, even more shocking. First of all there was the admission that releases of uranium oxide from corroding fuel cartridges in the 1950s were two hundred times higher than originally admitted. Then there was BNFL's acceptance that the total amount of plutonium discharged into the atmosphere over the years had been much greater that previously suggested. In

1984, BNFL said that atmospheric plutonium releases had been 67 gigabecquerels. Two years later the company revised this upwards to 174. But a paper submitted to the court by Professor Steve Jones, BNFL's head of environmental protection, finally put the figure of total plutonium releases prior to 1984 at a staggering 3,400 gigabecquerels. In other words, BNFL's original estimate of atmospheric plutonium emissions had been more than fifty times too low. This was all, of course, in addition to the three-quarters of a tonne of plutonium that had been dumped down Sellafield's pipeline into the Irish Sea – and which was now gradually coming back ashore.

Despite the alarming extent of Sellafield's environmental pollution, Martyn and his team maintained their focus on Professor Gardner's evidence because they believed it was stronger. They abandoned plans to call any environmental expert witnesses of their own, simply choosing to attack BNFL's experts instead. This strategy, which I am sure seemed the right one at the time, meant that the whole case effectively hung on the credibility of Gardner's hypothesis, which became known as Paternal Preconception Irradiation. BNFL devoted a great deal of effort to attempting to undermine Professor Gardner's work, which it said had been 'deliberately blurred' in a way which favoured his hypothesis. The company was supported by one of Britain's most eminent epidemiologists, Sir Richard Doll, who suggested that Gardner's study was biased and incorrect. Unfortunately, Professor Gardner, whose reputation had always been faultless, was in no position to defend himself. He died of lung cancer in January 1993.

After ninety days in the High Court in London and legal costs totalling at least £8 million, the judge, Mr Justice French, delivered his verdict on Friday, 8 October 1993. I went down south specially and, accompanied by my younger sister, Nina, and my mother, fought through the journalists and photographers on the street outside to get into the court room. Inside it felt cold and looked very strange, with all the benches and tables made of ancient, polished wood. But it was packed, and the atmosphere was tense and expectant. It took two hours of talking before Mr Justice

French got to the point. He said he had decided on the balance of probabilities that it had not been proved that the irradiation of fathers had been a material cause of their children's leukaemia. Martyn Day, Elizabeth Reay and Vivien Hope had, in other words, lost. Mrs Reay, a frail, elderly woman of seventy-three, did not get the £150,000 compensation that she had claimed for the loss of her ten-month-old baby girl and Ms Hope, who was twenty-eight, did not get the £125,000 she had claimed for her disability. They were both understandably disappointed, and, I think, rather shaken by the vulture-like attention of the media. Drinking coffee afterwards in Martyn's office, everyone was very depressed. But I refused to be downcast.

It seemed to me that simply by having the courage to mount the case in the first place we had won. We had received an enormous amount of publicity, enabling us to tell the world about the scandal of what had been happening around Sellafield. We had shown that, despite BNFL's best endeavours, there were some people in the local community who were not prepared to remain silent; who could not stand by while their husbands were irradiated at work, their environment irrevocably poisoned and their children killed. We were just ordinary people and we had sent shock waves through the nuclear establishment around the world, frightened the nuclear industry in Britain and shown up British Nuclear Fuels (annual turnover £1.1 billion) as petty and mean-minded. I was particularly disgusted by what BNFL's lawyers did immediately after Mr Justice French had finished delivering his verdict. They leaped to their feet to ask the judge to introduce what is known as a 'pools clause' in the agreement over legal costs. This meant that if ever Elizabeth Reay or Vivien Hope, whose costs had all been met by Legal Aid, received a financial windfall such as winning the football pools, it would have to be handed over to BNFL as a contribution to the company's legal costs. The request was granted.

BNFL argued on television that the £8 million spent in fighting and defending the case would have been better invested on trying to find a cure for leukaemia. This made me angry too, as it seemed to me that prevention is always better than cure. The court case was aimed at trying to determine the cause of the excess of childhood leukaemias around Sellafield. If it had succeeded, it would have been more valuable than any further research into cures, because action could have been taken to eliminate the cause.

Our hopes of being able to return to court in the short term were dashed when the same judge, Mr Justice French, turned down an application by Martyn Day to postpone for a year any hearing on Gemma and seven other cases for which Legal Aid had been granted, to allow further research to be completed. The judge agreed to BNFL's suggestion that the cases should be discontinued, but made it clear that a fresh action could be brought if new evidence linking Sellafield to childhood leukaemia emerged. In the meantime we lost our entitlement to Legal Aid.

In the next issue of the company newspaper, *BNFL News*, the front-page banner headline was '*CLEARED*'. BNFL's company secretary and legal director, Alvin Shuttleworth, was quoted as saying: 'With such a decisive judgement, the Legal Aid Board as well as the courts would appear to have concluded that BNFL's operations are not the cause of leukaemia in children in West Cumbria.' BNFL's next annual report also claimed that the court had 'cleared BNFL of the allegations that radiation from Sellafield had caused leukaemia in children'. The kindest thing to say about such claims is that they are misleading. There was no way that the court had 'cleared' BNFL of all responsibility for the leukaemias. It had simply decided, on the balance of probabilities and in the absence of supporting evidence, that Gardner's theory of Paternal Preconception Irradiation could not currently be blamed. It had agreed that the cluster of leukaemias near Sellafield could not be explained by chance, but it had concluded nothing – and was not asked to conclude anything – about whether or not environmental radiation from Sellafield could have been responsible. The argument is still wide open.

Since the court case finished, the scientific argument about the cause of the leukaemia cluster has rumbled on. Just ten days later, the government's Health and Safety Executive published a detailed study which in some ways supported Gardner's theory. The study found a 'strong statistical association' between the childhood leukaemias in Seascale and the radiation doses received by their fathers at Sellafield, but it found no evidence of such an effect in the rest of West Cumbria. It did not rule out as a cause either radiation exposure or the theory that the large influx of Sellafield workers into the area in the 1950s and 1960s could have introduced a cancer-causing virus (a theory known as 'population mixing'). The study's director, deputy chief inspector of nuclear installations Eddie Varney, said: 'We cannot find any single cause that satisfactorily explains what we see. It is difficult to deny a role for population mixing, but we find it hard to rule out radiation in the case of Seascale. But radiation alone cannot explain Seascale.'

A bewildering series of further studies, all of which have come to similarly tentative conclusions, have since been published. A study conducted by the Cancer Research Campaign's epidemiology unit at Oxford University, whose results were published in March 1993, found an apparent link between fathers exposed to radiation at two nuclear weapons plants in Berkshire – Aldermaston and Burghfield – and the high rate of childhood leukaemias in the local area. Another study done at Birmingham University, reported at the same time, showed an almost threefold increase in the rate of cancer amongst the children of people who worked with nuclear materials. In both cases the authors thought that their results tended to support the Gardner hypothesis. On the other hand Dr Leo Kinlen, also from the Oxford University unit, has written a number of high-profile papers which he said lent support to the population-mixing and viral theories and cast doubt on Gardner's work. Other studies – like one by the government's Committee on the Medical Aspects of Radiation in the Environment, whose findings appeared in September 1992 and another by Oxford University, Leeds University and the Royal Victoria Infirmary in Newcastle, which reported in November 1993 – just sat on the fence. They confirmed that there was a significant excess of childhood leukaemia near Sellafield that was unlikely to have been caused by chance, but were unable to offer any clear explanation as to why.

Other studies gave other insights. An exhaustive examination of

95,000 people employed by the British nuclear industry since 1945 – published in 1992 – found a statistically significant association between the incidence of leukaemia and prolonged exposures to low levels of radiation. The government's National Radiological Protection Board suggested that the risk of low-level radiation causing leukaemia might be twice as high as previously thought. A study by doctors at Lancaster Moor Hospital and a Cumbrian general practitioner, published in the *British Medical Journal* in November 1990, argued that the grandchildren of Sellafield workers had a high risk of developing a rare eye cancer that can lead to blindness. They reported three cases of retinoblastoma amongst the grandchildren of Sellafield workers where less than one would normally be expected. Three years later one of them, Dr James Morris from Lancaster Moor Hospital, wrote to the *British Medical Journal* pointing out that two more cases had been brought to his attention since the original report had been published, making the rate of eye tumours amongst the children of mothers living near Sellafield twenty times that expected.

There is more research under way, and of course more is necessary. But I doubt – at least in the short term – whether a causal link between Sellafield and the local excess of childhood leukaemias will become scientifically uncontroversial. It is safe to predict that there will be dozens more learned papers, some of which will tend to blame Sellafield and some of which will not. One aspect of future research, though, does concern me. In September 1994, a plush new £3 million scientific centre called the Westlakes Research Institute was opened near Whitehaven in Cumbria. Most of its research will be into the environmental and health effects of Sellafield, including possible causes of the raised incidence of childhood leukaemia. It already holds data on the radiation dose records and cancer rates of BNFL workers, past and present. According to its brochure, its mission is to be recognised 'as a scientific establishment of national and international repute'.

The problem is that Westlakes is almost entirely funded by British Nuclear Fuels. Virtually all the money for building and equipping the institute came from BNFL, and in 1994 the company sponsored 90 per cent of its research contracts. Most of the institute's senior research staff used to work for BNFL, including its director, Roger Berry (BNFL's former health and safety director), its chairman, Gregg Butler (former manager of BNFL's Springfields site near Preston), its business director, Tim Knowles (BNFL's former head of corporate affairs), and its director of environmental research, Steve Jones (BNFL's former head of environmental protection). It is regarded by some outside scientists as 'BNFL's in-house lab'. It may be that all these good people backed by BNFL money will one day discover the precise mechanism that connects Sellafield to childhood leukaemias. But I am not holding my breath.

Since Gemma was first diagnosed as having leukaemia in July 1987 I have spent a great deal of time reading, talking and thinking about radiation and Sellafield. I have learnt much, and doubtless have much more to learn. But I have come to some clear, and I hope informed, conclusions. There can be no doubt that radiation causes cancer, even at very low levels. Prolonged exposure to small amounts of radioactivity increases the risk of cancer, particularly cancer of the blood – leukaemia. This does not mean that everyone who receives such exposure will become ill. But it does mean that some people – perhaps only a few – will contract a disease that they otherwise would not have done. Broadly speaking, BNFL and the government's nuclear regulatory authorities accept that this is the case. That is why they will admit that certain releases of radiation could 'theoretically' increase the incidence of cancer in affected populations. The National Radiological Protection Board, for example, said in 1992 that planned emissions of radioactive krypton gas from Sellafield could cause two or three fatal cancers every year. As Steven once pointed out, if he had set up a business which killed two or three people every year, he would be in prison for murder.

The argument is over precisely what levels of radiation can be blamed for specific conditions in specific individuals. If one person is given a large dose of radiation and then goes on to develop cancer, it is relatively easy to prove cause and effect. But if thousands of people are given small extra doses and then four or five of them contract leukaemia, it is very difficult to prove a causal link. This is especially true, as in our case, where there is no way of really knowing exactly what levels of radiation people were exposed to in the past. I doubt whether we shall ever be sure of Steven's true exposure at Sellafield, and there is certainly no method of measuring in retrospect what all of us picked up on Cumbria's beaches. I understand the scepticism of some scientists when confronted with a statistical association between Sellafield and childhood leukaemia that does not conform to conventional understanding of how low doses of radiation affect people. But do we have to accept conventional understanding – which is, after all, only based on studies of Hiroshima and Nagasaki victims – as gospel?

I accept that it is always going to be hard to prove beyond any shadow of a doubt that Gemma's leukaemia was caused by Sellafield. But several things are clear to me. The science of radiation is relatively new, and there is much we still do not understand. The more we discover, the greater the risks turn out to be. It would not be surprising, therefore, if in a few years' time scientists uncovered a hitherto unknown health effect due to a particular type of radioactivity at very low levels previously considered safe. There are already some investigators who are suggesting possible new ways in which alpha radiation – the type that is emitted by plutonium – could damage our living cells. In these circumstances, it seems to me that the sensible way to behave is to assume that it is all dangerous. That means constantly questioning accepted notions of radiation safety and being prepared to abandon conventional scientific wisdom when there is good reason to doubt it.

No one really knows the cause of leukaemia, particularly chronic myeloid leukaemia. According to the Leukaemia Research Fund:

> Persons exposed to excessive doses of radiation, such as survivors of the atomic bombs at Hiroshima and Nagasaki and patients

> who have received radiotherapy for a variety of medical conditions, have a slightly greater chance than other people of developing Chronic Myeloid Leukaemia some years later, but for most patients radiation probably plays no part in causing the leukaemia. The possible involvement of other environmental agents such as drugs, chemicals or viruses has still not been determined.

Scientists know that patients with chronic myeloid leukaemia always have a mutant bone marrow gene, but they have no idea what causes it to mutate. It could be a combination of several different factors. A virus introduced by the arrival of a large number of people from a different area could make some people's bone marrow cells more susceptible to radiation damage. Chemicals such as benzine, which is contained in petrol, or others associated with microelectronics could help trigger or progress the change, as could some drugs. In such a state of ignorance, I think we all have to use our common sense. We know that radiation causes leukaemia. We know that more children than usual around Sellafield suffer leukaemia. We know that the environment around the plant has been contaminated with radioactivity. As far as I am concerned, this leads to one inescapable conclusion. Either directly or indirectly, on its own or in association with other agents, via paternal exposure, environmental pollution or both, radiation from Sellafield is responsible for children contracting leukaemia. Only a fool – and an arrogant fool at that – could carry on pretending there is nothing to worry about.

Unfortunately that is precisely the attitude that has been adopted by British Nuclear Fuels. I have never ceased to be amazed at the company's unshakable faith in its innocence, almost as if only its own scientists were incapable of error. BNFL always claimed that it was not the money that prevented the payment of compensation to leukaemia victims, it was principle. If so, it is a cruel principle. Given the weight of the evidence, given the common-sense conclusion that most people would draw, a compassionate company would have accepted moral responsibility. A company that cared about its public image would have agreed to settle the leukaemia cases before they came to court. That would have cost taxpayers considerably less than the £8 million they ended up spending and – following the pattern of the compensation scheme already agreed for irradiated workers – it could have been done without any admission of legal liability. By doing the decent thing, BNFL would have come out smelling of roses. Instead, there is a more pungent reek.

A similarly sour smell hung around the company's tacit support for attempts by leading Cumbrians to ban the filming and broadcast of Granada Television's drama-documentary about Gemma. The trouble started when Granada advertised in the local press for young girls who wanted to play the part of Gemma. Then in June 1993, when the film crew appeared on St Bees beach and erected some signs warning about the dangers of radiation simulating those erected by Greenpeace in 1983, all hell broke lose. An irate Conservative councillor, Norman Clarkson, tried to mobilise a convoy of vehicles to blockade the crew in their car park until they surrendered their film, but got there too late. He claimed that if the film was allowed to be screened it would do 'untold damage' to the economy of the local area. A spokesman for BNFL agreed that the programme should not be made, commenting that 'the tragic story of Gemma D'Arcy is not a suitable subject for entertainment'. The company wrote to Granada making the same point.

Two months later, local council leader Bill Minto chaired a special meeting in St Bees involving politicians from across the spectrum, business leaders, tourism officials and other local worthies. They demanded a chance to preview the documentary and angrily threatened to report Granada to the Independent Television Commission (ITC) if it was unfair. They were backed by the local newspaper, the *Whitehaven News*, which complained that people who live and work in West Cumbria would be seen as 'some kind of mentally subnormal beings'. The former deputy Conservative Prime Minister, Lord Whitelaw, went so far as to write to Granada, the Broadcasting Complaints Commission and the ITC saying that 'he could not accept the idea of any film of this sort being broadcast at this time'. His complaint, like all those that were made about the programme, was rejected. When BNFL's chief executive, Neville

Chamberlain, complained after the programme was broadcast about its 'highly charged' nature, Granada's chief executive delivered a robust response:

> I do not expect you to acknowledge the merits of *Fighting for Gemma* but I would ask you to accept that it was produced in good faith and in line with our normal high standards of programme making. To characterise it as 'the suffering of an innocent child making good television' is to impute a purely cynical motivation to us which is unfair.

The title of the programme, which was always scheduled to be broadcast after the court case had finished, was changed from *Justice for Gemma* to *Fighting for Gemma* in the light of the verdict. Lasting two hours, it was screened at eight o'clock in the evening of Wednesday, 10 November 1993 and was watched by around eight million people. I saw two previews, one arranged locally by the producers and one arranged by Martyn Day in the Little Gem Theatre in London just before the actual television broadcast. As soon as I saw the opening sequence of Gemma riding her bike and Steven taking photographs on the beach, accompanied by the song 'My Girl', I started to cry. But my tears were not of self-pity, rather of sympathy for the poor family on screen. I was irritated by some of the liberties that the script took with the timing of events, and sometimes impatient with the laboured way in which Martyn and his team explained what seemed obvious, but these were minor complaints. Basically I thought the programme was very fair, very good and very powerful. It conveyed the essence of what we had had the misfortune to endure. I revelled in the fame it would attract to Gemma's name. My daughter, as I had intended, was never going to become anonymous. Her brief life, her bitter experience, her avoidable death were never going to fade away.

Despite all my previous experience, I was not prepared for the onslaught that followed. Because Steven and I were in London at Martyn's preview, it was my sixteen-year-old sister, Nina, who received the dozens of telephone calls at home, most of them from well-wishers. There were a few unpleasant anonymous calls suggesting that we had been used and that Gemma's memory should be buried, which upset Nina. When we got back the next day we were greeted by a large bouquet of flowers from Granada Television, thanking us for our help. Then the local rumour mill went into overdrive, with the extraordinary suggestion that we had made up to £750,000 from the programme. For the record, all we ever got out of Granada, apart from a few cups of coffee and some fish and chips, was a £500 consultation fee for taking time off work to help the producers.

Then came the deluge of letters. There were a few nasty ones, all anonymous and nearly all of which we threw away. I suspect most of them were from local people, either Sellafield employees or their close relations. However much I tried to rationalise them, they hurt. How am I supposed to react when people take the time to write to me to tell me that I should shut up, that I am threatening to put people out of work, that I am hurting the feelings of others who have lost someone close? How can I remain rational when someone suggests that, because Gemma is dead, I should forget her? By accident, I did keep two of the less hysterical letters. 'Only those with sick minds could watch a child suffer or let it be shown,' said one. 'Please, Mrs D'Arcy, let Gemma rest in peace, and only then will you have peace of mind.' The other, which was signed by 'A Supporter of BNFL', took me to task for having the audacity to challenge the nuclear industry. 'West Cumbria would be in a sad state without BNFL. So would your family, friends and neighbours. Have you given any thought to this?' it lectured. 'Take a bit of advice. Get on with your life. You only come this way once, enjoy it. Your husband had a good living out of BNFL. You'll never win.'

Happily, the bad were far outweighed by the good, none of which were anonymous. There were so many that I never got a chance to reply to them. Often very personal, deeply sympathetic and hugely heartening, they were really important in helping me continue the struggle. I am for ever grateful to their authors, most of whom were ordinary mothers like myself. The following extracts are typical:

> I don't know if this letter will ever reach you, but I just had to write, as one mother to another. I watched the television programme tonight about your dear daughter Gemma. I am still crying now and I don't think a programme has ever affected me so deeply . . . Gemma's sense of humour and inner strength were fantastic, and she is an inspiration to many adults who treat life so lightly, and throw it away so easily.

> I have just been watching *Fighting for Gemma* and had to write and say how privileged I feel having 'met' Gemma through the programme. I lost my mother eighteen months ago and my two-and-a-half-year-old daughter was conceived while my husband had cancer. He also works at Sellafield. I live my life in fear living where we do.

> I have just gone through anger, hope, desperation, frustration and devastation in two hours. Dear God, what on earth did you go through? And what do you still go through every day? . . . I feel that in all these circumstances where giant companies have power and wealth, they can walk all over normal, everyday people. But eventually if enough people join together and are strong, they can at least start to rock the boat.

> You must carry on the fight for Gemma. The truth must out. She must not have died in vain. I admire your guts and determination to fight on. How proud she would be of you! Please don't give up. One day Gemma D'Arcy's name will trip off the tongue as the case that took on and beat the Big Guns!

> I want to let you know that I know that Gemma existed because tonight she has touched part of my life . . . I was born in Whitehaven . . . My three eldest children played on the beaches at Drigg and Seascale. I can remember having to jump over the

> discharges on the sand from Sellafield. It was crazy . . . I hope that your bravery in allowing this programme to be shown will make the British public think more carefully about Sellafield and nuclear power stations.

Sellafield, meantime, has carried on leaking. A leak of liquid plutonium on 8 September 1992 led to a reprocessing plant being shut down for seven weeks. Plutonium nitrate spilled into a hot steel-lined concrete cell and formed 'crusty lumps' on the inside. Scientists were worried that enough plutonium might congregate to set off an accidental nuclear chain reaction which would have caused a burst of radiation. The plant had to be closed down so that the contamination could be cleaned up. After investigating the incident, the government's Nuclear Installations Inspectorate (NII) said that the leak had only been spotted by good luck. Instruments which should have alerted plant operators failed to do so, and the problem was only noticed 'visually'. The NII was concerned that 'there weren't any lines of defence left'. BNFL originally told the NII that just 700 grams had leaked, but later upgraded this to 'several kilograms'. The incident was initially described as level one in the International Nuclear Event Scale, defined as an 'anomaly'. But when the full picture emerged, it was redefined as level three – 'a serious incident'.

On 10 February 1993, about one gigabecquerel – a very large unit of radioactivity – of radioactive dust was released into the atmosphere from a disused plutonium purification plant, showering local areas. Although the government insisted that the release was safe, it provoked an uncharacteristically angry outburst from one of Sellafield's best friends, the local Labour MP, Dr Jack Cunningham. He had been on an official visit to the site while the leak was taking place, but had not been told about it by BNFL – an oversight described by the Environment Minister, David Maclean, as 'a rather extraordinary discourtesy'. Dr Cunningham told the House of Commons the following week that there had been a 'totally unacceptable series of events' at the site. Two weeks later BNFL confessed that there had in fact been a second leak – three gigabecquerels of radioactive iodine from a reprocessing plant – around the same time.

Just two days later, on 27 February 1993, BNFL pleaded guilty in court to four charges of violating safety regulations at Sellafield – its third such conviction. Magistrates in Whitehaven fined the company £6,000 and awarded the NII, which brought the prosecution, nearly £11,000 in costs. The problem arose in April 1992 from the deliberate over-riding of a safety lock designed to prevent the inadvertent opening of a heavy radiation-proof door shielding a high-level nuclear waste store. Although the error was spotted and corrected before anyone was exposed to excessive radiation, the NII launched a prosecution because the incident was similar to another that had taken place the previous year. On that occasion the NII had warned BNFL to make sure that it did not happen again. BNFL had previously been convicted of moving irradiated nuclear fuel around the site without radiation detection equipment and for contaminating the beaches in 1983 (which I described in Chapter 1).

With such a poor record on top of the controversy over the child leukaemia cases, observers might have expected BNFL to do all that it could in the future to reduce its radioactive discharges. In fact they are set to increase dramatically. In December 1993, after twenty years of controversy, the government finally gave BNFL the go-ahead for a new £2.8 billion plant at Sellafield, known as the Thermal Oxide Reprocessing Plant or THORP. Over the next ten years THORP is set to reprocess spent fuel from nuclear power stations in nine different countries: Britain, Japan, Germany, Switzerland, Spain, Italy, Sweden, the Netherlands and Canada. According to BNFL, it will make a profit of £500 million over the same period. Like its predecessor reprocessing plants, it will discharge liquid radioactive waste into the Irish Sea and gaseous radioactive waste into the atmosphere. According to BNFL's THORP application to Her Majesty's Inspectorate of Pollution in 1992, the amount of plutonium put into the sea would triple over two years (from 1,080 to 2,997 gigabecquerels), as will levels of caesium 137. Emissions of ruthenium 106 and carbon 14 are set to rise eight times, while those of strontium 90 will leap ten times. Aerial emissions of radioactive materials like krypton 85 are scheduled for similar increases.

A report by the government's National Radiological Protection Board, revealed by the *Observer* in October 1993, estimated that radiation doses delivered by Sellafield to the world's population would almost quadruple after THORP started up. The report calculated that this could lead to several thousand cancer deaths over the next ten thousand years because of the persistence of two very long-lived radioactive substances that would be released – krypton 85 and iodine 129 – which 'circulate globally and therefore irradiate large numbers of people'. This official estimate was much higher than that previously calculated by scientists commissioned by the environmental group Greenpeace, who reckoned ten years of releases from THORP would eventually cause six hundred fatal cancers. At the same time a government advisory body, the Committee on Medical Aspects of Radiation in the Environment, warned that the proposed increase in radioactive emissions from Sellafield 'should be viewed with some concern'. Another government adviser, the Radioactive Waste Management Advisory Committee, cautioned that THORP could lead to Sellafield becoming the world's nuclear waste dump, with hundreds of tonnes of plutonium-contaminated waste from other countries being buried there.

Because of public concern over THORP, which was originally given the go-ahead after a long public inquiry in 1977, the government held two public consultation exercises, one in 1992 and the other in 1993, after the plant had been built. There were objections from ten nations, including Scandinavia and Ireland, 104 local authorities and nearly 90,000 individuals. Even America made clear its view that separating plutonium increased the risk of nuclear weapons proliferation. Despite this, all the Government did when it allowed THORP to proceed, was to place specific limits on uranium emissions and ask BNFL to produce annual reports on its discharges. It refused to hold another public inquiry. Greenpeace immediately took the government to court for allegedly breaching European law, but lost. As a result, Cumbria, Britain and the world are lumbered with a plant whose radioactive discharges are likely to kill thousands with cancer. The 'deliberate scientific experiment' started by Sellafield in the 1950s is continuing.

Some people might argue that this would be acceptable if THORP was fulfilling a useful function. But, as I argued in Chapter 4, reprocessing is a totally redundant technology, making nuclear waste more difficult to dispose of and producing an extremely toxic product – plutonium – that no one wants. Over the next ten years THORP is expected to process 2,670 tonnes of spent fuel from Japan, 2,160 tonnes from Britain, 970 tonnes from Germany, 420 tonnes from Switzerland, 50 tonnes from the Netherlands and a total of 140 tonnes from Italy, Spain and Sweden. This will produce about 55 tonnes of plutonium to add to the 40 tonnes of civil material that are already stockpiled at Sellafield, the ultimate destination of most of which is unknown. About 27 tonnes – perhaps fifteen shiploads – are expected to be taken back to Japan by sea for use in its fast breeder reactors, if they work.

But plutonium of course has another use – as a nuclear explosive. It is no longer a secret how nuclear weapons are designed, and there are no great technical problems involved in making them. The only thing preventing international terrorist groups from building their own nuclear bomb is the availability of plutonium. THORP could remove that barrier by making plutonium more easily available. It will also increase the risk of nuclear weapons spreading to more countries and encourage other nations to use their civil nuclear power programme to make nuclear weapons. This is precisely what the international community has been trying to prevent countries like Iraq and North Korea from doing. As a report compiled for the US Defence Department concluded in 1983, THORP will increase the danger of nuclear war.

I have never argued that Sellafield should be completely shut down. I just want it made 100 per cent safe – for the environment, for local children, for the world. It may be too late to do anything about the environmental crimes of the past which helped kill my Gemma, but there is much that can be done to prevent the same crimes being repeated in the future. I think giving the go-ahead to THORP risks sacrificing human lives and global security for a few Cumbrian jobs. What BNFL and the British government should accept is that reprocessing is a dangerous white elephant, an ancillary nuclear technology which may have seemed potentially useful in the 1950s – especially for military purposes – but which is out of place in the 1990s. It is certainly not an industry that should be sold into private ownership. For the sake of future generations, reprocessing should be phased out at Sellafield as it has been in most other countries in the world. This would not necessarily have any effect on the generation of electricity in nuclear power stations, as their spent fuel could simply be stored instead of being reprocessed. It would not leave Sellafield with nothing to do, as Britain would still face major long-term problems in handling the waste accumulated after forty years of nuclear power. But it might make the world a safer place to live in for the next millennium.

I also think that we do have to question whether we want to rely for our electricity on the radioactivity released by the splitting of the atom. Although nuclear power programmes are being enthusiastically pursued by a few countries like France, in most developed nations, such as Britain and Germany, they have ground to a halt. Nuclear electricity is not essential to meet our energy needs, which can be easily provided by a combination of energy conservation, cleaned-up fossil fuels and renewable sources such as the sun, wind and waves. Like Sellafield, nuclear power stations such as Three Mile Island in the USA and Chernobyl in the Ukraine have had accidents, in 1979 and 1986 respectively, which resulted in dangerous amounts of radioactivity being released into the environment. Although in normal operation nuclear reactors are not as dirty as reprocessing plants, they routinely create large amounts of radioactivity, including plutonium, in their cores. All of this has to be treated, stored or disposed of somehow – with or without reprocessing – causing an eternal risk of environmental contamination. The problem of radioactive pollution begins in every nuclear reactor. It will only finally be solved when they have all been shut down.

In 1993 Greenpeace invited me to attend an anti-nuclear

demonstration in the Netherlands, along with two other local mothers whose children had suffered and recovered from leukaemia, Lynn Marr and Janine Allis-Smith. I had never contemplated joining a protest before and had no idea what to expect. To be frank, I was a little apprehensive. We were taken to a packed meeting at Greenpeace headquarters in Amsterdam where a man was standing on a table explaining to everyone the plans for the following day. We had to get up at four in the morning, assemble at the Greenpeace offices and take a two-hour coach trip to a small power station called Dodewaard which was sending its spent fuel to Sellafield for reprocessing. Lynn, Janine and I were put up in a small bed and breakfast, but everyone else got what sleep they could in sleeping bags on the office floor. We were told not to drink too much as there would not be any toilet facilities at the site.

Just before we arrived at the power station, our coaches pulled off the road to enable the protesters to change into skeleton suits. When we reached the station's gates, they all quickly ran out and lay down all along the driveway, as if they had just died on the spot. It was an impressive and rather ghoulish sight, all the more admirable for the fact that the temperature was well below freezing. When the plant's senior management arrived around eight o'clock, they were not pleased. The only way anyone could get into the plant was by stepping over scores of 'dead' bodies. Greenpeace demanded a meeting to put their concerns to managers, which was at first angrily turned down.

Initially I did not know what to think. I talked to one of the protesters, a Dutch doctor, who told me he was deeply worried about the health effects of the reprocessing of Dutch fuel at Sellafield. I admired his determination to act on his beliefs. I looked at the human skeletons laid out on the ice-cold ground and realised that that was what they were all doing. They were using their bodies to protest peacefully about the contribution that their country's nuclear reactors were making to Sellafield's environmental crime. They were acting to try and prevent pollution from a plant 400 miles away killing any more children like Gemma. I began to admire what they were doing. I decided that I could not just stand by and watch.

The plant manager, Mr Arnold, who had been growing increasingly irritable about the disruption being caused to normal operations, was nearby. I approached him, asking if I could have a word. He turned his back and started walking away. I pulled out a picture of Gemma behind her red-line prison in the Royal Victoria Infirmary and shouted at him: 'Can I give you this photograph? It is a picture of a child suffering from leukaemia. It is a picture of my daughter. It is her that these people are fighting for.' He turned to face me, reluctantly took the photograph and put it in his pocket without a word. He subsequently agreed to meet with Greenpeace and to hold a separate meeting with Lynn, Janine and me.

Confronting Mr Arnold across his desk, with two Dutch MPs listening in, was a bizarre experience. But I think we made our point, and he certainly seemed to listen. He did not agree with our contention that radiation from Sellafield had caused our children's illnesses, but as a father and grandfather himself he sympathised with our feelings. At one point he took Gemma's photograph out of his pocket, stared at it and then looked up at me. 'I gave you the picture so that you could relate to a person, not a statistic,' I told him. 'It shows my little girl enduring terrible suffering. It shows her losing her happiness, losing her childhood, losing her life. She was my daughter and very precious to me, but she is only one of many victims of Sellafield.'

Of course the protest did not stop the Netherlands sending spent fuel to Sellafield. But it did achieve something – publicity for the issue, problems for the power station and – perhaps – a few second thoughts amongst its workers and managers. It was strange to realise that the further you travel from Sellafield, the more concerned people seem to be. It was chastening to appreciate the truly international scope of BNFL's business. It was immeasurably heartening to know that, wherever I was likely to go in the world, I would not be alone in my fight. I like to think that, in a small way, I reached the heart of Mr Arnold. All change has to begin with such small steps.

Someone important from a foreign nuclear company listened to me, understood what I was saying and did not pour scorn on my views. That may not be much, but it is far more than British Nuclear Fuels has ever done.

Afterword

When I became pregnant again in 1992, my feelings were confused. I felt guilty at my selfishness, alarmed at my recklessness and deeply happy at the thought of creating another new life. I desperately wanted another baby and Richenda desperately wanted another sister, but I was worried sick about the risk of leukaemia. Experts told me that the chances of two cases occurring in the same family were extremely remote. But I distrusted experts, especially those who spout such statistics. After losing Janine, I was also nervous about the pregnancy itself, and insisted on regular check-ups if I felt anything was not quite right. This time, to give them their due, doctors sprang into action whenever I suggested there might be a problem – and there were a few.

When I was six months pregnant, my back started to ache on a train journey home from London. I dismissed it at first, assuming it was just the normal stress of pregnancy. But then I experienced shooting pains in my womb, and had to go into hospital for a check-up. I started losing liquid and was sent to see a specialist in Newcastle who warned Steven that, if the baby was not born at once, my life could be endangered as well as the baby's. The specialist said there was a risk of septicaemia, the blood poisoning that had finally killed Gemma. We agreed that the baby should be delivered as soon as possible, and I took some tablets to help her lungs develop. In Newcastle, with Steven present, Samina was born by Caesarian section on 13 December 1992. Nearly three months premature, she weighed just 2lb.

Like Richenda, she lived her first six weeks in an incubator in a special care ward. I had decided that she was not going to survive, so for the first few days I put up a barrier between us. I tried to express my milk rather than breastfeed her. I refused to hold her. Then, when Steven came on a visit, the nursing sister took us both to see her. She told us we could cuddle her if we liked. Steven held her first, and then she was passed to me. I stood awkwardly, holding this tiny wriggling being in my hands, refusing to look at her. Sister took some photographs, and then leaned over and whispered in my ear: 'Pull down the wall, Susan, she's going to be fine.'

I looked down and, for the first time, really saw her. My tears started to flow, and I fell in love with her. She was my baby daughter, and I had to take care of her as I had taken care of Gemma. Gradually, she grew bigger and stronger. She was sent back from Newcastle's special care ward to our local hospital so that we could visit her every day and night. The hospital gave us one scare when they suddenly sent her back to Newcastle for emergency checks – just like Gemma – but there turned out to be nothing wrong. She eventually came home on 2 February 1993 – exactly a month before she had been due to be born – and thrived. When she was eighteen months old we took her to see a consultant, who expressed concern about how little and pale she looked. He took a blood sample, like the hundreds that had been taken from Gemma, and we suffered a week of anxiety before we knew the results. I had to ring the haematology department myself to find out that she was fine.

As I write, she is nearly two years old, and still doing well. Although smaller, frailer and fairer, she looks like Gemma. She is beginning to behave the same way too, driving us crazy with her curiosity, astounding us with her cheek and making us laugh at her jokes. She toddles around this kitchen, narrowly avoiding the table legs, grinning hugely just like Gemma used to. But she is not Gemma, and never will be. She is her own person, deserving of her own unique love. She cannot – as some people have suggested – replace Gemma. She can remind us of her, help us remember her with a smile, but she is no reincarnation. We have told her about Gemma and she recognises her. When we took her to Gemma's grave, she bent forward and kissed her picture on the headstone. I do not suppose I shall ever escape the fear that she could succumb to the same disease that killed Gemma. But at this moment, I am optimistic.

Richenda, who at fourteen is growing into a beautiful young woman, loves Samina dearly and helps me look after her. She shows her the photograph of Gemma in her locket and tells her about her other sister. While I was writing this book, Richenda was asked by Channel 4 to make a short 'child's eye' documentary on how she felt about Sellafield. She went and interviewed workers and managers at the plant, and she sat in our living room interviewing me. That was the hardest part, especially when she asked whether I thought about her when I was in hospital looking after Gemma. I said I did, and that started the tears. Richenda has not made up her mind about whether radiation from Sellafield is to blame for Gemma's death. She knows my views, but she knows equally that I will not impose them on her. Her friends and teachers have made her aware that there is another point of view.

When her film was broadcast, she invited viewers to make up their own minds. I was very proud of her. I heard her talk more about Gemma than ever before:

> Gemma was a joyful, happy child. Everyone loved her. She was very cute and cheeky and had this way of talking people into doing what she wanted. She was a real kid, not an angel. She could be a right little madam. We used to fight like cat and dog. Then one of us would turn round and say: 'I love you.'
>
> When I went to see her in hospital, she looked like a different person. She'd put on weight and her hair was falling out, but she was still very cheeky. I had to put on a gown, a hat and a mask to see her. She'd say: 'Hello, clumsy. Mind my drip-stand,' because I am always knocking into things. All her dolls were lined up and she had put up a sign saying: '2p to guess the name of the dolls.' It was always in the back of my mind that she would die, but as long as she breathed the next day, I didn't think it would happen.

I was at my Auntie Tina's when she died. Nina and I were in bed. We were talking about it, saying what would happen if Gemma died and that we would still have each other. Then my uncle came in and we heard him being sick in the bathroom. And then he said: 'She's gone.' I went into the other room and cried on my own.

I used to go to Gemma's grave every day and spend all my pocket money on flowers. I went because someone had said I ought to go there to see my sister. Now I realise I don't have to. I can talk to her anywhere. I only go when I'm in a happy mood and I say things like: 'You should see Samina now. She's started talking.' Samina being born was the happiest time since Gemma died.

My elder sister Tina has now started her own business – a café in Whitehaven. 'Gemma was a lovely little devil,' she wrote. 'She had spirit, spunk and laughter. She had tears, pain and suffering. All of these things died with her. I owe a lot to Gemma and her illness. My priorities have changed. I used to worry about next month's fuel bills before I had paid last month's. Now I know that money and material things are not important.'

Nina, my younger sister, who is now seventeen, wrote a school essay recounting her feelings about Gemma. 'Nobody understood me when I did not cry at Gemma's funeral. But when I had seen her on that hospital bed crying and in pain, that's when I cried. To see her lying painless and quiet in her coffin was almost a relief.' Nina, like me, is sure that Sellafield is to blame and has promised to carry on my fight should anything ever happen to me.

Steven, who as ever keeps his feelings mostly to himself, has been out of work since February 1991, helping to look after the children. I doubt if he will ever work at Sellafield again. I am working as a waitress in Tina's café, and driving a clapped-out old Skoda. We still never have enough money, and have not been on a proper holiday since we went to Disneyland. I keep getting invitations to appear on television – British, German and Japanese – which I invariably accept because each is another opportunity to continue the fight for Gemma.

We have not moved from this council house in Cleator Moor, where Gemma lived for the last half of her life, because it is full of her memories, her shadows, her ghost. It is like a kind of monument to her. I do not think at the moment that we shall ever move. I know some people think we are crazy to stay here, given all that has happened. But it is our home. It is where all my friends and relatives live. It is where the fight to keep Gemma's name alive has to be fought. If I moved to Manchester or London, I have no doubt I would get more support for my stance from local people. But it would not mean as much as it does here. We have made one change, however. We do not go down to the beach any more.

Sitting here at my kitchen table every evening writing all this down has surprised me. I feel the better for it, a little soothed, a little healed. I have lived again through all the emotions, all the highs and lows, of my short bitter-sweet time with Gemma. I have conjured her magical personality out of the darkness, watched her skip through the light, and then confined her back into the dark again. The emotions I felt at the time have all returned in force, sometimes almost blocking out the present. But now at the end – after all the joy, pain and sorrow – it is my anger that burns.

I do not want you to mourn Gemma: I want you to celebrate her. I do not want you to lament her passing: I want you to rail at the injustice she suffered. I do not want you to cry for her: I want you to fight for her. If her death is to mean anything, it must mean change – a fundamental change in our attitude towards the nuclear industry. For such change to come about, ordinary people like you and me have to speak up for what we believe in. There could be no better memorial for my daughter.

SELECT BIBLIOGRAPHY

ARNOLD, Lorna, *Windscale 1957: Anatomy of a Nuclear Accident*, Macmillan, 1992.

AUBREY, Crispin, *Thorp: the Whitehall Nightmare*, John Carpenter Publishing, 1993.

BLOWERS, Andrew, David Lowry and Barry Solomon, *The International Politics of Nuclear Waste*, Macmillan, 1991.

BOND, Martin, *Nuclear Juggernaut: The Transport of Radioactive Materials*, Earthscan, 1992.

CUTLER, James and Rob Edwards, *Britain's Nuclear Nightmare*, Sphere Books, 1988.

MAY, John, *The Greenpeace Book of the Nuclear Age*, Gollancz, 1989.

McSORLEY, Jean, *Living in the Shadow: the Story of the People of Sellafield*, Pan, 1990.

The Observer, *The Worst Accident in the World, Chernobyl: the End of the Nuclear Dream*, Pan Books/William Heinemann, 1986.

PATTERSON, Walter C., *Nuclear Power* (second edition), Penguin, 1986.

PRINGLE, Peter and James Spigelman, *The Nuclear Barons*, Michael Joseph, 1982.

SUMNER, David, Tom Wheldon and Walter Watson, *Radiation Risks*, Tarragon Press, 1991.

ANTI-NUCLEAR ORGANISATIONS IN BRITAIN

Cumbrians Opposed to a Radioactive Environment (CORE)
98 Church Street
Barrow-in-Furness
Cumbria
LA14 2HT
Tel: 01229 833851

Friends of the Earth (England, Wales and Northern Ireland)
26–28 Underwood Street
London N1 7JQ
Tel: 0171 490 1555

Greenpeace
Canonbury Villas
London N1 2PN
Tel: 0171 354 5100

Safe Energy Journal
Friends of the Earth (Scotland)
72 Newhaven Road
Edinburgh
EH6 5QG
Tel: 0131 554 9977